ZOE MINISTRIES INTERNATIONAL

HOW TO HEAR GODS VOICE
IN CHRIST

STUDY GUIDE

Rev. 9/13

ACKNOWLEDGMENTS

ZOE Ministries International is dedicated to training, equipping and sending believers into the world to minister by the leading of the Holy Spirit. This ministry helps build the body of Christ and encourages God's people to use their gifts and talents for His glory. It is for this purpose that this publication has been compiled by the leading of the Holy Spirit and the input of many people. ZOE Ministries wishes to thank them for their support, time, and talents in contributing to this Study Guide. We give our Lord all the praise and glory for this work!

HOW TO HEAR GOD'S VOICE — IN CHRIST
CONTENTS

COURSE OUTLINE

Lesson 1 **INTRODUCTION**
Class Articles: *Vessels In The Potter's Hand*, S. Sasser
Vessels Of Honor, Channels Of His Power, K. Henry

Lesson 2 **LOVE AND UNITY**
Renner: Preface, Chapters 1 and 2
Scripture: **Ephesians 4:3; John 15:1–17**
Assigned Articles: *One Body, One Spirit*, J. Aldrich
As The Wheel Turns, S. Shank

Lesson 3 **MOTIVE GIFTS**
Renner Chapters 3 and 4
Scripture: **Romans 12:1-8**
Class Articles: "Three Biblical Groups of Gifts" ZOE Ministries
Perception and Serving Motive Gift Tests, D. and K. Fortune
(a separate booklet)
Assigned Article: *Laity: Called, Gifted, Trained, Sent*, J. Garlow

Lesson 4 **MOTIVE GIFTS — PERCEPTION AND SERVING**
Renner: Chapters 5 and 6
Motive Gifts Scripture: **Romans 12:6-7**
Perception Motive: John the Baptist - **Luke 3:2-20**
Serving Motive: Martha - **Luke 10:38–42; John 12:2**
Class Article: Teaching and Exhortation Motive Gift Tests
Assigned Article: *No Christian Is An Island*, J. Guest

Lesson 5 **MOTIVE GIFTS — TEACHING AND EXHORTATION**
Renner: Chapters 7 and 8
Motive Gifts Scripture: **Romans 12:7–8**
Teaching Motive: Apollos - **Acts 18:24–28; 1 Corinthians 3:6**
Exhortation Motive: Barnabas - **Acts 4:36; 11:22–26; Acts 14:1–26; 15:2–3, 35–41**
Class Article: Giving and Administration Motive Gift Tests
Supplementary Reading: *Using Our Gifts*, C. Bates

Lesson 6 **MOTIVE GIFTS — GIVING AND ADMINISTRATION**

Renner:	Chapters 9 and 10
Motive Gifts Scripture:	**Romans 12:8**
Giving Motive:	Abraham - **Genesis 13 and 14**
Administration Motive:	Joseph - **Genesis 37, 39, 41**
Class Article:	Mercy Motive Gift Test
Assigned Articles:	*Seeking More Of The Spirit*, M. Bickle
	The Gifts, The Calling And The Anointing, J. Stocker

Lesson 7 **COMPASSION MOTIVE GIFT**

Renner:	Chapters 11 and 12
Motive Gifts Scripture:	**Romans 12:1–21**
Compassion Motive:	Good Samaritan - **Luke 10:25–37**
Study Help:	"Motive Gifts Comparison" ZOE Ministries
Class Article:	Motive Gift Tie Breakers
Assigned Article:	*Fresh Oil*, G. Headley

Lesson 8 **GETTING ACQUAINTED WITH THE HOLY SPIRIT**

Renner:	Chapters 13, 14, 15 and 16
Scripture:	**John 14, 15 and 16**
Study Help:	"The Holy Spirit—Who Is He?" ZOE Ministries

Lesson 9 **THE INTIMACY OF THE TRINITY**

Assigned Articles:	"Outline to Accompany the Trinity Teaching" ZOE Ministries
	"Trinity Diagram" ZOE Ministries
	The Trinity, D. Jenkins
	Quench Not The Holy Spirit, V. Synan
	Jesus—The Heart Of God, D. Lindsay

Lesson 10 **GIFTS OF THE SPIRIT — REVELATION GIFTS**

Renner:	Chapters 17 and 18
Scripture:	**1 Corinthians 12**
Word of wisdom:	**Matthew 22:15–22**
Word of knowledge:	**John 4:1–42**
Discerning of spirits:	**Acts 13:4–12**
Study Help:	"The Gifts of the Holy Spirit—The Revelation Gifts," D. Iverson
Assigned Articles:	*Learning To Be Spiritually Discerning*, J. Dawson
	Cultivating The Spirit's Gifts, J. Deere
Supplementary Reading:	*Discerning Of Spirits*, J. MacNutt

Lesson 11	**GIFTS OF THE SPIRIT — POWER GIFTS**	
	Renner:	Chapters 19 and 20
	Scripture:	**1 Corinthians 13**
	Gift of faith :	**1 Kings 17:1–16**
	Gifts of healings:	**Matthew 20:29–34**
	Working of miracles:	**Matthew 14:22–33**
	Study Help:	"The Power Gifts", D. Iverson
	Assigned Articles:	*The Gift Of Faith*, M. Chavda
		Gifts Of Healings, M. Pearson
		Working Of Miracles, R. Bonnke

Lesson 12	**GIFTS OF THE SPIRIT — VOCAL GIFTS**	
	Renner:	Chapter 21
	Scripture:	**1 Corinthians 14**
	Prophecy :	**Luke 2:25–35**
	Different kinds of tongues:	**Acts 2:1–12**
	Interpretation of tongues:	**Daniel 5**
	Study Help:	"The Vocal Gifts", D. Iverson
	Assigned Articles:	*Prophecy: God Speaks Through Ordinary People*, K. Clement
		Guidelines For The Prophetic Word, J. King
		The Gift Of Prophecy, J. Wimber
		Tongues And Interpretation, J. Hayford

Study Materials:

1. Bible, any translation
2. Rick Renner, *The Dynamic Duo*, Creation House, Lake Mary, Florida, 1994
3. Don and Katie Fortune, *Discover Your God-Given Gifts, Adult Questionnaire,* Discover Your Gifts, 20126 Ballinger Way #120, Shoreline, WA 98115-1117 www.discoveryourgifts.org.
4. Various Articles in the Study Guide
   a. Class Article—to be read in class
   b. Assigned Article—to be read in preparation for class
   c. Supplementary Reading—optional—will not be discussed in class
   d. Study Help—optional—for the student's use in studying Scripture

A REMINDER TO ZOE COURSE PARTICIPANTS:

What ZOE Is!

1. A ministry that provides training for disciple-making.
2. Participatory courses where all are encouraged to share and contribute.
3. A situation where the leader (facilitator) decreases and the participants increase.
4. A drawing out of ministry gifts and preparation for the Lord's calling on individual lives.
5. A time when one can grow in the understanding and appreciation of others' gifts.
6. A safe environment in which an individual can feel comfortable to practice operating in his or her gifts.
7. A time of understanding the heart of the Father and applying that to one's life.

What ZOE Is Not!

1. A traditional Bible study.
2. A course where the leader speaks and the people take notes.
3. A place where people can air their opinions or gripes.
4. A place where people can discuss church doctrines.
5. A time when "weird" ministry happens.

A Reminder to ZOE Facilitators:

"A ZOE course is not just a Bible study, I am a facilitator and coach, not a teacher"

It is our desire that the Lord Jesus Christ be glorified in all that is said and done in ZOE courses. We wish to foster an understanding of the operation of His Holy Spirit and to yield to His workings.

MAIN PRINCIPLES

Lesson 1: God has fashioned each of us as a vessel for His use. As God's vessel, we contain His glory and the knowledge of Him. We should become the best vessel we can be and allow God's life and love to pour out of us to others.

Lesson 2: God calls us to abide in Christ and live in love and unity with one another. As we do this, we will be witnesses of God's love to the world. As we have communion with the Holy Spirit, we allow Him to make us into the image of Christ Jesus and to keep us together in unity. Remember, Jesus is the true vine and we are the branches, but the Holy Spirit is the sap that brings life and causes us to bear fruit that remains!

Lesson 3: God has given each of us in-born gifts that we should use to build up the body of Christ. Discovering how God has gifted each of us can promote unity because then we can better understand and help one another.

Lesson 4: People with a perception motive gift perform the function of the eye for the body of Christ, while servers perform the function of the hands.

Lesson 5: People with the teaching motive gift perform the function of the mind for the body of Christ, while exhorters act as the mouth.

Lesson 6: People with a giving motive gift perform the function of extended arms, while people with the gift of administration serve as the shoulders of the body of Christ.

Lesson 7: People with the compassion motive gift perform the function of the heart of the body of Christ. Each of the motive gifts reveals to the world a different aspect of God's character. When we understand each other and the way God made us, we can complete each other, not compete with each other.

Lesson 8: An exciting and fulfilling relationship with the Holy Spirit is available to all believers. We are called into a deeper realm of God through daily communion with the Holy Spirit. It is out of a relationship with Him that God will pour out His powerful love on a hurting world.

Lesson 9: We need to get to know who the Holy Spirit is and how He works together with the Father and with Jesus. Then we can draw closer to Him and cooperate with Him as He works through us to bring glory to God.

Lesson 10: We can work together in partnership with the Holy Spirit. As we lay aside our fears and our own plans, the Holy Spirit will tell us what to do and say. We are privileged to participate with God as His Spirit moves upon us with words of wisdom, words of knowledge and discerning of spirits.

Lesson 11: We are privileged to participate with God as His Spirit moves upon us with the gift of faith, gifts of healing and the working of miracles.

Lesson 12: When the Holy Spirit moves upon us with His vocal gifts, we can make evident God's specific word for our time and place.

HOW TO HEAR GOD'S VOICE—IN CHRIST

PARTICIPANT'S RESPONSIBILITIES

I. Course Preparation

A. Read the assigned scriptures and come prepared to share in the course.

    1. Ask the Holy Spirit, **"Open my eyes that I may see wonderful things in Your law." Psalm 119:18** You may be very familiar with the assigned Scriptures, but the Lord is very faithful and can give you "fresh manna."

    2. Look at the Main Principle for the course and apply the Scriptures. Ask yourself the following questions:
        a. How does this Scripture apply to the lesson?
        b. How does this Scripture apply to my life?
        c. What do I need to do to apply this Scripture to my life and to the lives of others for God's glory?

B. Read the assigned chapters or pages in the book and come prepared to share in the course.
Note in your book any thoughts related to the Main Principle for the lesson.

C. Read the assigned articles and come prepared to share in the course.
Note any thoughts related to the Main Principle for the lesson.

D. Maintain a journal—a valuable tool in God's hands.
As you learn to hear God's voice and keep a record of His speaking, you will become more aware of what He is saying to you and how He wants to work through you. See the article "Journaling—A Good Way to Hear God's Voice."

E. Spend time in prayer.

    1. Prayer is valuable preparation for these courses. The more time you spend with the Lord, the more you will come to know Him.

    2. Spend time with God <u>daily</u>! God shows no partiality—what He has done for others, He will do for you! Growth will come as you respond to God's Holy Spirit at work in your life.

II. Course Participation

A. Training is active! You will be encouraged to **take part in the course discussions and the prayer and ministry time.**

B. You will have the opportunity to **lead the discussion** of the assigned reading as you feel comfortable. No one will be forced to lead—only encouraged!

JOURNALING – A GOOD WAY TO HEAR GOD'S VOICE

What Goes Into a Journal?

1. Your thoughts—impressions, insights, hopes, fears, goals, struggles
2. Your feelings—both positive and negative
3. Your prayers and answers to prayer
4. Excerpts from Scripture and other reading that God seems to be highlighting for you

How to Journal

1. You may choose to use a spiral binder or a hardback blank book, or anything that you can take with you easily on trips.
2. Journal every day, if possible, during the time that you read Scripture and pray. Record in it insights that the Lord gave you that day or the day before.
3. You may want to keep a separate section in your journal for prayers or excerpts from your reading.
4. Write directly to God as if you were talking to Him or writing Him a letter.

The Benefits of Keeping a Journal are Many

1. Journaling fosters a readiness to hear from God. Personal communion with God takes place as you write out your thoughts and feelings, and record the insights and impressions He gives you.
2. As you read God's Word and record your insights about Scripture, God is faithful to provide the admonitions, encouragement and guidance that you need.
3. Prayers become specific as you place them in print. In addition, God gets the glory when you review your journal and see your prayers have been answered.
4. Journaling helps clarify your thinking. Fears and struggles are more clearly defined so that they can be dealt with.
5. During times of discouragement, it can help to look back over your journal and see God's faithfulness and your progress in spiritual growth.

GUIDELINES FOR LEADING A CLASS DISCUSSION

1. Prayer

As you study the assigned material, ask God for insights. Ask Him to show you the main points to be discussed and questions to ask to aid the discussion. Come a few minutes early to the course and pray with the Facilitators before the course begins.

2. Maintain Control of the Discussion

After the class has been turned over to you by the Facilitators, you are to maintain control of the discussion.

a. Do not allow one or two participants to dominate the discussion time.

b. Stick to the subject. God may give you many insights, but keep the discussion related to the Main Principle of the lesson.

3. Work Within the Allotted Time

For a 2½ hour class:

    Approximately 30 minutes for the book

    Approximately 50 minutes for the Scripture discussion

    Approximately 15 minutes for the articles

      (Allowing 20 min. for the Facilitators to lead the prayer/ministry)

For a 1½ hour class:

    Approximately 20 minutes for the book

    Approximately 30 minutes for the Scripture discussion

    Approximately 10 minutes for the articles

      (Allowing 10 min. for the Facilitators to lead the prayer/ministry)

ZOE courses focus on what God says through the Bible. Be careful not to spend too much time on the book or articles, which are provided only as supplements to the Scriptures.

4. Encourage Discussion

Class members should be prepared to share insights that the Lord gave them while they read the assigned material. You may need to draw out these insights by asking questions.

a. Begin with a *launch* question, a broad question that can be answered in a number of different ways by anyone in the group.

b. Then use *guide* questions, which are short questions that keep the discussion moving in a direction that is related to the Main Principle of that lesson. Life application of the principles found in the assigned reading should be a focus during some part of the discussion.

c. To close the discussion time, summarize very briefly the main points of the discussion.

May God bless you as you study and pray in preparation for the class. We will be praying for you as you prepare. We love and appreciate you. ~*The Facilitators*

LESSON 1

MAIN PRINCIPLE

God has fashioned each of us as a vessel for His use. As God's vessel, we contain His glory and the knowledge of Him. We should become the best vessel we can be and allow God's life and love to pour out of us to others.

DISCLAIMER

The articles that follow have been chosen to give you, the reader, a broader perspective on many of the issues presented in the course. All the ideas in these articles do not necessarily represent the views of *ZOE Ministries International*. However, we pray that as you read and study, you will glean a sense of what is in the author's heart. At all times we need to ask the question, "Does this line up with the Word of God?"

VESSELS IN THE POTTER'S HAND

by Sam Sasser

God spoke to Jeremiah in an incredibly unique metaphor: "Arise and go down to the potter's house, and there I will cause you to hear My words." Then I (Jeremiah) went down to the potter's house, and there he was, making some thing at the wheel. And the vessel that he made of clay was marred in the hand of the potter; so he made it again into another vessel, as it seemed good to the potter to make.

Then the word of the Lord came to me, saying: 'O house of Israel, can I not do with you as this potter?' says the Lord. 'Look, as the clay is in the potter's hand, so are you in My hand, O house of Israel!" (Jer. 18:2–6).

THE VESSEL OF HONOR

In examining the Word carefully, I found seven vessels created on the potter's wheel. The first vessel is found in II Timothy 2:20, 21: "But in a great house there are not only vessels of gold and silver, but also of wood and clay, some for honor and some for dishonor. Therefore if anyone cleanses himself from the latter, he will be a vessel for honor, sanctified and useful for the Master, prepared for every good work." A *vessel of honor*

took a great deal of time to fashion and mold. It was pressured into usability by the potter and then placed in the kiln and heated to a point that assured its durability. It was the vessel most purchased from the potter. The vessel was filled with water and placed at the door of either a private dwelling or the temple so a person might quench his thirst or wash his hands or feet. In the Church there are many vessels of honor. They are filled daily so they can be poured out on someone else.

THE VESSEL OF MERCY

The second vessel mentioned in the scriptures was called the *vessel of mercy*. "That He might make known the riches of His glory on the vessels of mercy, which He had prepared beforehand for glory" (Rom. 9:23). The major difference between the vessel of mercy and the vessel of honor is that the vessel of mercy is filled at the wellsprings daily and taken to the city square. There a stranger can go and find a source of refreshment. We can be vessels of mercy, filled with the waters of refreshment for the thirsty stranger. He may not find his way into a church service. He needs to come in contact with somebody with vibrancy in his life, right there in the

marketplace.

THE CHOSEN VESSEL

The third vessel was called the *chosen vessel*. Before Saul of Tarsus became the Apostle Paul, he was blinded by heavenly light on the road to Damascus. God told Ananias—a vessel of honor—to go and pray for Paul to be healed. When Ananias questioned God, He commanded: "Go, for he is a chosen vessel of Mine to bear My name before Gentiles, kings, and the children of Israel" (Acts 9:15).

Imagine Ananias' shock when he heard Saul of Tarsus was a chosen vessel! A chosen vessel was the best the potter could make. It was a vessel that had yielded to the potter's pressure and been put into the kiln. During its time in the kiln beautiful colors had come forth. The chosen vessel is the only vessel on which the potter put his entire name. Every other vessel bore his mark, but the chosen vessel bore his full name. After the vessel was finished, the potter did something strange: he took the chosen vessel into a side room and set the vessel gently on the dirt floor, and left it there in the darkness for three to five years. At the right time, for the proper occasion, the potter chose one of them, knowing it would never bring him dishonor. It was the best his hands could make.

God has molded and forged many believers. He places them in the fires of life, and their beautiful colors are exposed. Then He takes them to the storage room and sets them on the ground in total darkness until the time comes when the Potter opens the door and He bends over and picks up that vessel. He holds it in the sunlight and says, "Child, it's your turn to give your life away."

THE CLEAN VESSEL

The fourth vessel was called the *clean vessel*. Isaiah 66:20 says: "... Bring an offering in a clean vessel into the house of the Lord." The clean vessel was a vessel that had been molded and made just like any other. But because of overuse, it had become tainted and was no longer called a vessel of honor. It was just a clean vessel.

Overuse can taint a person more quickly than anything. Once every quarter, priests in the Temple gathered the clean vessels that had been used for offerings and took them to the potter's shop to be restored as vessels of honor.

The potter did four things in the restorative process. First, the vessel was emptied of all its contents. For the believer, that is never an enjoyable time, but it is imperative.

Second, the vessel was scraped inside and out with strong files and brushes to loosen the plaque. When God is scraping on the inside a person can hide it; but there is no hiding the outside scraping. God scrapes inside and out—loosening everything that should not be there.

Third, the lips of the vessel were reset. Because of overuse, the lips widened and did not pour accurately. They needed to be reset and remolded. Many times, our lips utter words that should not be spoken. Our lips need to be brought back to the hand of the Potter to be reshaped.

Fourth, the vessel was put into the fire one more time. That's where we want to draw the line. We don't want to go back into the fire. But it is the fire that makes a clean vessel into a vessel of honor.

THE VESSEL OF DISHONOR

Fifth was the *vessel of dishonor*. This was the Judean garbage can. Pockmarked and ugly because of air in the clay, it was purchased only to accommodate garbage. The dregs of life were poured into it every day until it had a stench. Then it was carried to the far corners of the owner's fields and thrown away. It was called an abominable vessel.

THE BROKEN VESSEL

Sixth was the *broken vessel*. David said, "I am like a broken vessel" (Psa. 31:12). This vessel was cracked at the lip in the fire of the kiln. When the potter took it out and found that crack, he did not throw it away; he labored with it. In the fields around Jerusalem there was a little insect— a tick that gorged itself on the backs of bulls and goats. The blood of this tick was the strongest glue known in the Holy Land. The potter would take the tick between the thumb and forefinger and crush its body, mixing its blood with the clay. Then he would take that blood-soaked powder and rub it into the crack.

In our humanity, we sometimes crack and do not look like we should in the midst of the fire. We come out of the fire cracked. But the Master Potter does not throw us away. Instead, with His blood He begins to remake us.

After the potter repaired the crack with the blood, he took the broken vessel and put it back into the fire one more time. If it cracked again, he would repeat the process 12 to 15 times.

THE VESSEL OF WRATH

However, if that broken vessel continually rejected the blood and did not adhere to it, the potter had no choice but to label it a *vessel of wrath*, the seventh vessel. "What if God, wanting to show His wrath and to make His power known, endured with much longsuffering the vessels of wrath prepared for destruction" (Rom. 9:22).

At the end of the day, the potter would take the broken vessel—the one that refused to adhere to the blood and had become a vessel of wrath—to the wall of Jerusalem and cast it over into the Potter's Field. The broken pieces were good for nothing but to scrape the wounds of lepers at night. It was the potter's loss.

The Master Potter is fashioning our lives for service. Let us allow Him to mold, shape and fire us for His glory! †

—Adapted from a message given at CFNI in Dallas.

Sam Sasser served as a missionary, church planter and evangelist in the Marshall Islands and Samoa from 1960 until his death in 1995.

VESSELS OF HONOR, CHANNELS OF HIS POWER

by Kent Henry

It was just a few years ago that the Lord gave me a prophetic song concerning direction for our lives and some of His purposes for our future. It stated that He had called us apart to live as vessels of honor and channels of His power. We are literally a people sanctified, set apart to be available for His divine use.

This prophetic song was a picture statement to help us visualize some of the higher purposes to which we are called in God. The challenge is to look beyond our everyday definitions of being vessels, and grasp, by the Spirit, the fullness of understanding this call. As a baseline motivation for living, being a vessel of honor and a channel of His power is one of our greatest honors and highest priorities.

GOD'S TREASURE IN EARTHEN VESSELS

II Corinthians 4:7 says this: *But we have this treasure in earthen vessels, that the excellency of the power may be of God and not of us.* A prime focus then of being vessels is to flow in God's power showing forth in an excellent way the treasure of the Lord Jesus Christ deposited within us. This covers both the spiritual side of the

kingdom of God (i.e., prayer and Bible study) and the practical side of our lives (i.e., family and work-related matters).

This scripture should help us understand that God has not been looking for perfect vessels, rather vessels that are yielded and have made themselves available to change. God knows the abundance of our frailties and weaknesses. All the more do we see, as does the world, that this power that works in us is of God, as well as the excellency and the glory of that power.

Webster's definition of "vessel" includes these three characteristics: "being a receiver or a repository of some spirit or influence; a utensil for holding something as a bowl or pitcher; in botany, a tube or canal serving to conduct water." These definitions list out a few of the simple, yet mighty aspects of being used by the hand of the Almighty.

1. **We are now the repositories of His Holy Spirit, at least in part.** Jesus sent the Paraclete, the helper, the one who will lead us and guide us, as an earnest deposit on your vessel. *Now He who prepared us for this very purpose is God, who gave us the Spirit as a pledge* (down payment, earnest deposit) (II Corinthians 5:5).

2. **We are holding-reservoirs and then we become those canals from which can flow an abundant supply of His living water.** *Now on the last day, the great day of the feast, Jesus stood and cried out, "If any man is thirsty, let him come to Me and drink. He who believes in Me, as the scripture said, 'From his innermost being shall flow rivers of living water'"* (John 7:37–39).

STAGNANT POOLS OR FLOWING RIVERS?

Rivers here in this passage is the Greek word *pot-am-os'*. It includes within its definition these other words: "river, a current, a brook, a stream or a flood, a freshet (as drinkable), i.e., running water." This may indicate a major problem many Christians are having today with their walk in the Lord. The flow of the Spirit has been replaced by a stagnant pool in place of being a vessel full of drinkable running water.

The scriptures are full of references that God's people would be like springs or fountains. Gushers of living water will flow out of your belly or, rather, out of your innermost being. This begins to help us sum up the power source for both being a vessel and a channel for the Lord. It is the Holy Spirit who is present daily to flow out of us in streams and rivers that others may taste and see that the Lord is good.

Now in a large house there are not only gold and silver vessels, but also vessels of wood and earthenware, and some to honor (noble use or great occasions) and some to dishonor (lowly or ordinary use, even menial service). Therefore, if a man cleanses (purifies) himself from these (sins), he will be a vessel for honor (noble purposes), sanctified (set apart and consecrated), useful to the Master, prepared for every good work (II Tim. 2:20–21).

VESSELS FOR HIS PURPOSES

Vessels of honor! God has actually given us a place of honor in His house. A place of honor to bring pleasure to His heart and a great blessing to the earth. The purpose of this place is to be prepared and useful for the Master's work. This reminds me of the scripture in I Corinthians 6:20: *For you have been bought with a price* (vs.19 *you are not your own*): *therefore glorify God in your body.*

This position, more so this calling, carries with it the requirement of walking in integrity and the fullness of godly character. But it should also speak to you concerning the importance of your individual life as a person which the Lord desires to use in a great way. It maybe hard to believe now, but you have a profound purpose and are of vital importance in God's plan. You are a person of destiny.

Stretch out this year for new things in the Lord Jesus. Think anew and afresh of the possibilities of the Holy Spirit using you as a vessel of honor, and a channel of His great power. No looking back now, only pressing forward for the prize of this high calling. Glory!!!

—Kent Henry has served as pastor, music director, Psalmist Magazine founder, and worship conference leader. He currently heads Kent Henry Ministries and is dedicated to teaching churches about the need for a culture of prayer and justice.

Reprinted by permission: Psalmist Magazine

MAIN PRINCIPLE

God calls us to abide in Christ and live in love and unity with one another. As we do this, we will be witnesses of God's love to the world. As we have communion with the Holy Spirit, we allow Him to make us into the image of Christ Jesus and to keep us together in unity. Remember, Jesus is the true vine and we are the branches, but the Holy Spirit is the sap that brings life and causes us to bear fruit that remains!

ASSIGNED ARTICLE

ONE BODY, ONE SPIRIT

by Joseph C. Aldrich

In heavenly math, one + one = one. When a butcher cleaves, he or she makes two out of one. When a husband cleaves, he makes one out of two. In the church, all become one.

Galatians 3:28 tells us that "there is neither Jew nor Greek, there is neither slave nor free, there is neither male nor female; for you are all one in Christ Jesus" (NKJV). All we need to do is act like we're "all one."

Unity is a miracle. If the church of Christ stood together as a harmonious community of brothers and sisters where love and peace ruled, it would be such a unique phenomenon in our egotistical culture that everyone would be forced to acknowledge that it is divine in its origin.

Unity is a victory. All unity has a perceived outcome that somehow overcomes the gravitational pull toward disunity. We see it in athletics, in battle and in business. If the cause is grand enough, rewarding enough, thieves will unite in common cause. Unfortunately, much of so-called "unity" centers around personal gain at the expense of others. It's called greed.

When "Thy kingdom come" becomes "my kingdom come," the blessing of God goes somewhere else. There are two essential "joinings" that constitute the foundation for Christian unity. Without these joinings, it is doubtful believers would ever come together in common cause. Because of these two joinings, they have no option. That is, they have no option if they want to please Him.

Through the new birth, you are supernaturally joined to Christ. This is the first joining. Jesus used some organic metaphors to describe this reality:

///

GOD'S DESIRE IS THAT THERE

BE NO DIVISION IN THE

BODY - THAT ITS PARTS HAVE

EQUAL CONCERN FOR ONE

ANOTHER

///

He is the Vine, we are the branches. He is the Groom, we are the bride. He is the Head, we are the body.

The night of His betrayal, Jesus talked about this joining with His disciples. "At that day," He told them, "you will know that I am in My Father, and you in Me, and I in you" (John 14:20). Sounds like we are all tossed into a divine blender of some sort! Every believer is "in Christ." The implications are significant.

"Therefore, if anyone is in Christ, he is a new creation; old things have passed away; behold, all things have become "new" (2 Cor. 5:17). The "new" comes when this union bears fruit, when the branches draw sustenance from the vine, when the body responds to the head.

A Presbyterian and a Baptist are joined to the same vine, they're engaged to the same Lord, they're in the same sheepfold, they're stones in the same building, they're indwelt by the same Spirit. They may even study the same book and sing the same hymns. Isn't that adequate reason to get along?

The imagery is not of one tree trunk (vine) nourishing just one branch. The life of God flows to myriad branches. God has no "only child."

There's a second joining. The first is vertical between God and us. The second is horizontal between believers themselves. Through the baptism of the Spirit, we are joined to the body of Christ. We are sovereignly placed into the universal church made up of all who have received Christ as Savior. "For by one Spirit we were all baptized into one body—whether Jews or Greeks, whether slaves or free—and have all been made to drink into one Spirit" (1 Cor. 12:13).

November 1992, Charisma

One body, one Spirit. It's believers united to Christ and each other whom God is calling to unity—those who lift up the name of Christ in the different communities of faith.

Some want out because they're different and proud of it. But the Scripture says, "If the foot should say, 'Because I am not a hand, I am not of the body,' is it therefore not of the body?" (1 Cor. 12:15). The Presbyterians have no basis for feeling superior to the Independent Bible Church. Slam!

Others want out because they don't need anyone else. Paul's answer? "The eye cannot say to the hand, 'I have no need of you'" (1 Cor. 12:21). The charismatic can't say to the Baptist, "I don't need you." Slam!

Like it or not, we're "members of one another." If one part suffers, every part suffers with it; if one part is honored, every part rejoices with it (1 Cor. 12:25–26). Furthermore, we're *interdependent*. We need each other. And the world needs us to be biblical in our support and concern for each other. God's desire is that there be no division in the body—that its parts (that's all of us) have equal concern for one another.

We can be thankful that we're joint heirs with Christ as a result of His sacrificial love. With Christ as the Head of a diverse group of believers, we must—as a body—stay focused on our common Goal. Only then will our message of love permeate the world.

—Joseph C. Aldrich has served as the head of Northwest Renewal Ministries, an organization dedicated to helping local churches bring revival to the U.S. Pacific Northwest. He is the author of Prayer Summits (Multnomah).

Reprinted by permission: Charisma Magazine and Strang Communications Company.

November 1992, Charisma

ASSIGNED ARTICLE

AS THE WHEEL TURNS

by Steve Shank

My three-year-old daughter was lost in her Play-doh world. I stood behind her, unseen, as she carefully squeezed and shaped the lumps of clay into saucers, cups and pots. Probably preparing to entertain royalty, I thought. Who could guess what kings and queens would soon be feasting at her table.

Suddenly, without warning or explanation, she smashed her fairy-tale creations. The hands that had carefully fashioned delicate "china" cups now pounded them just as easily back into a multicolored blob. And it didn't seem to faze her. She just slid from her chair, scratched her nose, and headed to the sink for a drink.

So much for the creations of Play-doh Land. Their three-year-old Queen had played with them until she got tired and then—wham—back to a blob. There was nothing they could say.

We human pots tend to give our Creator a little more flak, despite Isaiah's warning: "Woe to the one who quarrels with his Maker—an earthen-ware vessel among the vessels of earth! Will the clay say to the potter, 'What are you doing?' Or the thing you are making say, 'He has no hands'?" (Isa 45:9 NAS) The Lord deals patiently and redemptively with his children, and is not into smashing his creations. But that doesn't negate the fact that he could if he chose to.

As Creator and Owner of everything, he can do whatever he wants. He's not accountable to anyone. He doesn't have to explain any of his actions. He has unbridled, unlimited, unilateral power and authority.

It is God's mercy, not our own virtue, that has kept us on the potter's wheel. But mercy leaves little room for presumption. We're in the hands of The Sovereign God, the Holy One—and that's exactly where humility begins.

WHO'S IN CHARGE?

No question cuts more accurately between pride and humility. Humility admits that we're not in charge, admits that there is one higher than we are who has a plan for our life which he expects us to obey. Pride, on the other hand, talks back. Pride assumes we have rights—even before God. Pride sits on the spinning potter's wheel and thinks that it's the Potter who revolves around the pot! Pride forgets who is serving whom.

The proud abound in unfounded confidence and self-importance. Minutes before the space shuttle Challenger exploded in 1986, a priest was asked to pray for the operation. A NASA official leaned over and said, "You just pray for the weather and NASA will take care of

the rest." Less than 90 seconds after takeoff, seven astronauts had spiraled into oblivion.

The fact is, our society is fueled by arrogance. Pride is genetic. So when a person becomes a Christian, he must ax this self-confident, self-governing arrogance and learn the way of humility.

For Americans, nothing is harder. But humility isn't just a good idea. It isn't just one of many virtues in God's grab bag of character traits—it is the urgent, non-negotiable need of our day. Humility is the gateway to grace and favor from God. Pride, on the other hand, stonewalls God's grace and causes him to resist us. And take it from King Saul or stubborn Pharaoh: you don't want God working against you.

It's amazing to read that Jesus, the omnipotent ruler of the Universe who "upholds all things by the word of his power" (Heb 1:3 NAS), described himself as "gentle and humble in heart" (Mt 11:29). Think about it: God is humble. When we see this amazing virtue of our Lord, we'll see our own pride in its proper light. Silly. Stupid. Arrogant. Like pots arguing with the potter.

THE ART OF SELF-DEFENSE

Pride enjoys looking good in

the eyes of other people. In its concern about what others think, pride tempts us to defend our image and reputation. Yet we deceive ourselves if we try to stake our personal identity on physical traits, talents, accomplishments, titles, or money. That only makes us more insecure. The truth is, security grows in direct proportion to humility.

A tremendous freedom awaits the humble. We've got to understand how finite we are. Each of us is just one among billions of tiny bleeps on time's monitor. On an eternal scale, we are here and gone in an instant. None of us is indispensable. Anything we do and are for God is an unmerited privilege.

By our union with Christ, however, we have inestimable value in the eyes of God. We can stop striving—what great news! (It never impressed God anyway.) We are complete in Christ! Having nothing to defend, we have nothing to lose. We can strip off our pride and joyfully don the servant's apron.

IT IS GOD'S MERCY,

NOT OUR OWN VIRTUE,

THAT HAS KEPT US ON

THE POTTER'S WHEEL.

Humility is not a "worm complex." As we surrender our hearts in response to God's holiness and authority, we become more secure than ever.

GOOD CLAY

How can we grow in humility so that we're soft and pliable in the Potter's hands?

Decide. Humility is not a feeling, nor is it a timid, spineless personality. It's a conscious, deliberate choice. When Peter wrote, "Humble yourselves ...under God's mighty hand" (1 Pe 5:6), he didn't add, "wait till the mood strikes you." Humility is a decision within our control, and wisdom dictates that we humble ourselves daily.

Surrender. Humility obeys. Humility takes the argument and competition out of us. Humility breaks the unbridled stallion in us called "my way" and enables us submissively to embrace all of God's will. God doesn't owe us an explanation of his purpose, though we can and should ask for grace to fulfill his wishes.

Submit. God's kingdom is a hierarchy. He has established authority on earth, both secular and spiritual, as he sees fit. Though we are all equal in worth, we are not all equal in responsibility or gifting. "Some are apostles, some prophets" (Eph 4:11)—God distributes gifts as he chooses, and he hasn't asked for our opinion.

It's one thing to submit to God; it's something altogether different to submit to the gifts and authority of others. This cuts us at the nerve. Yet humility requires that we defer to one another; be accountable to one another, admit our need, and acknowledge another's greater measure of anointing and ability. Independent Christians who wield authority without being under authority are dangerous.

Be assured that God has anointed some individual—and an imperfect one, at that—to serve more effectively in an area than you ever will. Admit it to yourself; affirm it to him or her. It's good medicine.

Admit. Now is the worst time in history to be a know-it-all. Not only are they difficult to get along with, but know-it-alls flirt with the very attitude that puts a cap on future growth and often leads to deception.

Even though they have strong convictions, humble Christians remain quick to listen and slow to speak. Recently, I had breakfast with a man of national stature in ministry, a man whose counsel I sought. But before I could tap his wisdom and experience, he asked for my opinion: "What is God up to? What is he saying to you?" The humble man constantly seeks to learn God's ways more accurately. He always sees himself as a student, even if he is in a position of teaching others.

Those walking in humility depend on hearing God for themselves, yet realize they may not always interpret things wisely, accurately, or completely. Consequently, they are not threatened when their views are questioned. In fact, they welcome input. They draw their confidence from God, curbing the tendency to be satisfied only with what seems right in their own eyes.

As a pot myself, I am grateful that the Master Potter has kept me on the wheel, working patiently on my imperfections rather than starting with a brand-new blob. But the benevolent hands molding my life are also the holy hands of the Lord God Omnipotent—and that reminds this pot to watch himself.

—Steve C. Shank has been an author, teacher, world traveler, church planter, Bible College founder, and Pastor for over 30 years. He has spent most of his adult life training and equipping believers in Bible schools and churches around the world.

Reprinted from People of Destiny Magazine.

LESSON 3

MAIN PRINCIPLE

God has given each of us in-born gifts that we should use to build up the body of Christ. Discovering how God has gifted each of us can promote unity because then we can better understand and help one another.

THREE BIBLICAL GROUPS OF GIFTS

I. The Ministry Gifts (The Five-fold Ministry)—Ephesians 4:7–16

These are callings into which a person is **appointed by God/Jesus**—usually into full-time service. Their purpose is to **equip the saints** until they reach unity and maturity.

Each of these callings can be represented by one finger on your hand.

A. The **Apostle**—one who is sent
Position on the hand: The **thumb**—It touches all fingers just as an apostle's ministry touches all components of the five-fold ministry.
Scriptural example: Paul in **Galatians 1:1**

B. The **Prophet**—foretells the future
A true prophet's words are correct and his predictions will come to pass.
Position on the hand: The **pointer finger**—He points to the future or to the past, or calls people to repentance.
Scriptural example: Agabus in **Acts 11:27–28**

C. The **Evangelist**—travels proclaiming Christ
Position on the hand: The **middle finger**—He stands above the others as a soul winner. His words convict sinners and encourage believers.
Scriptural example: Philip in **Acts 8:4–8, 26–40**

D. The **Pastor**—protects and oversees the church
Position on the hand: The **ring finger**—He is "married" to his flock.
He loves, feeds and, when necessary, corrects them.
Scriptural example: Timothy in **1 and 2 Timothy**

E. The **Teacher**—clarifies truth for the church
Position on the hand: The **little finger**—He brings balance to the rest of the five-fold ministry by teaching from the Scriptures.
Scriptural examples: Priscilla and Aquila in **Acts 18:24–26**

II. The Spiritual (Manifestation) Gifts —1 Corinthians 12 and 14

These are manifestations of the Holy Spirit as He **moves upon believers** to empower them. They are supernatural gifts administered by the **Holy Spirit** for the common good, using whom He chooses at the time of need.

A. Three **revelation** gifts: Word of wisdom
Word of knowledge
Discerning of spirits

B. Three **power** gifts: Gift of faith
Gifts of healings
Working of miracles

C. Three **vocal** gifts: Prophecy
Different kind of tongues
Interpretation of tongues

III.   The Motive Gifts—Romans 12:6–8

These are **placed within us by God** at conception.

A. The motive gifts are not like the **ministry gifts** which **Jesus gives**, to which some people **are called**.

They are not like the **spiritual gifts** the **Holy Spirit manifests** as He **moves upon** a believer for a time and purpose.

Motive gifts are **placed within** each individual at conception, along with the faith to develop and use that gift.

B. The term "motive gift" is not a scriptural word, but it describes those gifts that move out from our inner being. Our motive gift is what *motivates* us and interests us. It is the reason behind what we do. It helps to describe how we view things.

C. Motive gifts show our God-appointed positions in the body of Christ. Discovering your motive gift can help you more fully understand what God wants you to do.

D. Examining these gifts helps us better understand the God-appointed positions of others with whom we live and work. This can contribute to greater love and unity.

1. Perception (Prophecy)

2. Serving

3. Teaching

4. Exhorting

5. Giving

6. Administration

7. Compassion (Mercy)

LAITY: CALLED, GIFTED, TRAINED, SENT

by Jim Garlow

God makes no distinction between secular and sacred. Those are perceptions we have. God regards all work as sacred as long as it is done unto Him for His honor and His glory.

In the year A.D. 325, the famous Council of Nicene defined the Church as "wherever the bishop is." The word bishop means "overseer" or, effectively, the pastor.

The problem with that definition is that it ruled out about 99% of the Church. The Church is comprised of all of God's people. Ephesians 4:11, 12 is the clarion call to the revolution of lay ministry. Verse 11 talks about those who are apostles, prophets, evangelists, pastors and teachers—the five-fold ministry. Verse 12 tells us why God ordained or established these functions or offices or giftings: to equip all of God's people for their work of ministry so that the body of Christ will be edified or strengthened.

My commitment to lay ministry came as a result of my doctoral studies in the area of church history. I studied the Wesleyan revival in England during the 1700's. It splashed over to America by the 1720's and was called the Great Awakening. In England, only about 40 Church of England or Anglican priests were sympathetic to this revival. So Wesley began to train and equip lay persons.

He trained over 653 lay preachers. 57% stayed with him until his death or theirs, whichever came first.

There are several distinct features of the Wesleyan revival which apply directly to the dynamics of lay ministry.

The first one is that lay people, biblically perceived, are *called* to the ministry. The concept is that ordinary people under the anointing of God can do extraordinary things. Those who are in Christ Jesus have been called into the ministry. The function or direction in which He takes believers varies from person to person. Frances Ayers, an Episcopalian, says, "If you're in Christ, you've been called into the ministry. You may be surprised by that statement, pleased, alarmed, antagonistic, acquiescent, scornful or even enraged. Regardless of how that statement strikes you, if you are in Christ Jesus, you have been called into the ministry."

We have been called to be a "kingdom of priests." A priest is simply an intermediary between God, Who passionately loves the world, and a lost world that desperately needs to know about that compassion. Israel didn't grasp that. The Church, too, has struggled with the concept. We're called to be the conduit, the pipeline through which God's Spirit and Word flows out to the world; we're to be a "kingdom of priests."

The Church is comprised of the King's own personally selected priests. Is the title of priest only for those who are seminary-trained, ordained or have a Bible-college degree? No. It's for all who are in Christ Jesus. If you are a believer, you are a part of the kingdom of priests.

Two words in the Greek are fascinating to me: *laos* and *laikos*. The word *laikos* means "a person who is not trained in an academic discipline." The word *laos* means "the people of God especially chosen for a profound work." It intrigues me that *laikos* is the word used by laymen in our churches—a word which never appears in Scripture.

> "THOSE WHO ARE IN
> CHRIST JESUS
> HAVE BEEN CALLED INTO
> THE MINISTRY."

On the other hand, the word *laos* appears repeatedly. If you're in Christ Jesus—the people of God—you are especially chosen for a special task.

This distinction made by so many between clergy and laity is invalid. The New Testament recognizes leadership and authority, but nowhere in Scripture do we find the concept that some are ministers and the rest of us are simply to be the inactive recipients of whatever leadership does. God says if you're in Christ Jesus, you're called to the ministry.

There's a move today to liberate people to ministry. I wish this move were going faster than it is. Our nation and our world desperately need all of us. Thomas Gillespie, President of Princeton Theological Seminary, says, "This revolution that we all desire, for lay people to take their role seriously, will never happen unless laity are willing to move up, clergy are willing to move over and all God's people together are willing to move out." Elton Trueblood, in his early nineties, says it this way: "If every lay person would come to understand who he is in Christ Jesus, we would have nothing short of a revolution overnight in our country."

The second distinct feature of the Wesleyan revival which applies to lay ministry is that biblically perceived lay people have been *gifted* for ministry. That means they have the capacity to see things happening in the realm of the supernatural, That means God ordains the release of His gifts through them, producing results which cannot be explained. Some don't take it seriously that they have been supernaturally gifted by the Spirit of God. But God has profoundly endowed His people with gifts. Throughout Church history when the gifts of the Holy Spirit have been emphasized, there was a greater use of laity. That was because of the understanding of the believer's role and calling before Christ. On the other hand, when the gifts have been deemphasized there has also been a massive de-emphasis on ministry done by the common, ordinary believer.

If the premise of biblical gifting is taken seriously, Christians will assist one another in finding their gifting areas. They will help each other find areas of ministry which call for their gifts. They will also help each other realize which areas of ministry they are not gifted in. That will reduce the burnout or frustration rate that's so prevalent in our churches.

We need to take the blinders off and see all the ways God can use us. Some people feel they have nothing to contribute to the cause of Christ, but the truth is that every human being has much to give. One little lady couldn't sing or teach or do any of the things we think of as ministry. But one day she looked out of her apartment in the city of Milwaukee, and saw people standing at a bus stop. She saw how cold and frustrated they were. She said, "I can make a difference in the name of Jesus." The next morning she took freshly baked cookies and hot coffee to the bus stop and fed the people. She did this day after day with no charge. They wondered why she was doing this, expecting some kind of catch. She said, "I'm doing it in the name of Jesus." This woman found a place where she could fit in and make a difference in the world.

We could reduce the frustration and feeling of emptiness many lay persons experience if we taught them to select ministries based on gifts they have. Many times a new Christian comes into a church excited and wanting to help, expecting to do things like they did in the book of Acts. But the person is assigned to some meaningless committee, and a few years later the life of Jesus has been drained away.

Too often instead of finding out what a person's gifting is and where he or she can maximize that giftedness, the person is assigned to an available "slot" in the institutional "machinery." Consequently, the joy of Jesus drains away because he or she is being asked to do things that he or she is not gifted to do. Every-body can do something profound for the Lord. We're all called and we're all gifted.

The third feature of the Wesleyan Revival applicable to lay ministry is that biblically perceived laity is to be *trained* and *equipped* for ministering to others. Most people don't understand that the purpose of the local church is to be a training and equipping center. It is not primarily a place of oratory. It is not primarily a concert hall. It is fundamentally to be an equipping and mobilization center.

The letterhead I received from a pastor about 15 years ago said, "The Ministers: The People of the Congregation." Underneath that it said, "The Equippers of the Ministers," and there it listed the pastoral staff. This pastor understood the role of apostles, prophets, evangelists, pastors and teachers according to Ephesians 4:11-12. They are to build up, strengthen and equip all God's people for their work of ministry. And it's the ministry of believers which edifies the body of Christ.

The laity are *called* to the ministry, *gifted* for ministry and need to be *trained* for the ministry. Each local church should restructure and reorganize itself to be a mini-seminary, a mini-Bible college which focuses on equipping and mobilizing believers to carry forth the Gospel to those in its sphere of influence.

And finally, we come to the fourth concept: sent into ministry. We are sent with "ambassadorial status," as a representative of Christ, for the purpose of accomplishing a clearly defined mission. Laity, biblically perceived, is *commissioned* for service. Just as pastors are ordained, so laity needs a type of recognition service as well, validating their "ministerial status."

The most important thing is not the number of people who *come* to our churches, but how many *go out,* equipped and mobilized, ready to make a difference. The bottom line is, how many are consciously, deliberately understanding that they are plainclothes officers in the Jesus revolution, infiltrating the pagan public with the only tool which will ultimately conquer the hearts of humankind?

It takes more than just having training classes in a church to make it a "high-functioning-laity" church. It takes an inexplicable excitement about doing Christ's work—a desire, a hunger, an energy of the Spirit flowing. And that can only happen when people understand who they are and what they've been called and gifted to do.

—Adapted from a message given at CFNI in Dallas.

Jim Garlow is an author, commentator, historian, cultural observer and Senior Pastor of Skyline Wesleyan Church in San Diego, California. Dr. Garlow has appeared on numerous U.S. television news shows and is heard daily on over 800 radio outlets in his one-minute historical commentary called "The Garlow Perspective."

Reprinted by permission: Christ for the Nations, CFNI, P.O. Box 769000, Dallas, TX 75376-9000, 800-933-2364.

LESSON 4

MAIN PRINCIPLE

People with a perception motive gift perform the function of the eye for the body of Christ, while servers perform the function of the hands.

NO CHRISTIAN IS AN ISLAND

by John Guest

THOUGH OUR SOCIETY SEEMS TO ENCOURAGE INDIVIDUALISM, PAUL CLEARLY TEACHES WHAT WE ALL CAN GAIN THROUGH FELLOWSHIP WITH ONE ANOTHER.

John Guest was born in Bristol, England, 52 years ago. His father died when he was 7, and he grew up with no religious background. His passion in life was to become a world-class soccer player.

When he was 18, he attended a Billy Graham Crusade. He went forward to accept Jesus Christ as Savior. "It was like stepping out of the London fog into the sunshine," he says.

In the late '60s he began missionary tours in the United States, eventually landing in Pittsburgh, Pennsylvania, and accepting the pastorate of St. Luke's Episcopal Church. During the past decade his church has more than quadrupled in size while other parishes in the same diocese have lost members.

Guest has become a leader in the Episcopal renewal movement as he is known for his in-depth teaching. Gleaning wisdom and spiritual insights, he takes his readers on a tour of Philippians in his new book This World Is Not My Home. *Creation House plans to release the publication later this month.*

Here, with permission, we have selected an excerpt from This World Is Not My Home. *In it Guest delves into Philippians to glean insight about fellowship.*

English poet John Donne once said, "No man is an island, entire of itself; every man is a piece of the continent, a part of the main; if a clod be washed away by the sea, Europe is the less ...."

Going back further, to the first century, we see that Paul also had something to say about people, particularly Christians, being "a part of the main." This theme appears again and again throughout Philippians.

Paul sees the church as a fellowship of citizens who work *together* for a cause, who fight together with camaraderie of army buddies. The kingdom of heaven is not meant to be a loose confederation of island individuals but a unified group committed to the welfare of each other. The only cell in the human body that does its own thing is the cancer cell. It's on its own timetable; everything it does is in disharmony with the rest of the body; and ultimately it destroys everything in its path.

Large pockets of the contemporary American church seem to have a different view from Paul of what the kingdom of God is all about. They like to sit in a pew—or in their living rooms—and watch as someone on a platform sings or prays or preaches. The church becomes like a movie theater where a performance helps an audience temporarily escape the rest of the world. People come and sit, expecting a certain amount of privacy and anonymity while God encourages them through the preacher.

Just as the Untied States is becoming a nation of armchair athletes, it's becoming a nation of pew polishers. I'm reminded of that description of an American football game: 11 men out on the field in desperate need of a rest and 50,000 people up in the stadium in desperate need of exercise. In a similar way, in too many churches the pastor and a small band of helpers are exhausted while most of the congregation sits and takes it all in.

Repeatedly, when Paul was in need, the Philippian church had sent him money, without any appeal from Paul himself.

At the same time, the Philippian church had sent him more than physical, monetary aid. Epaphroditus, one of their members, had traveled from Greece to Rome to help and support Paul in prison. Being

October, 1988 Charisma

LESSON 4

under a sort of house arrest, it seems, he could probably receive guests freely. So for some time, this Epaphroditus was at Paul's side as a servant.

For Epaphroditus this was no small sacrifice, as Paul tells us in Philippians 2:25–28 (RSV): "I have thought it necessary to send to you Epaphroditus my brother and fellow worker and fellow soldier, and your messenger and minister to my need, for he has been longing for you all, and has been distressed because I heard that he was ill. Indeed he was ill, near to death. But God had mercy on him, and not only on him but on me also, lest I should have sorrow upon sorrow. I am the more eager to send him, therefore, that you may rejoice at seeing him again, and that I may be less anxious."

Paul is sending Epaphroditus, who has been sick unto death, back home so that his family and friends will see for themselves that he is in good health.

There's such a wonderful give and take in the relationship Paul has with his friends in Philippi. He had introduced them to the good news. In appreciation they had remained loyal to him through his hard times. Now he, out of concern for them, was sending back home the man they had sent to his aid.

The love here is circular: Each party is making sacrifices for the well-being of the other. Each party is giving and in turn receiving help from the other. What does Paul call this? A "fellowship of suffering."

No, you may say, you don't want to think of this kingdom of God on earth as a fellowship of suffering saints. But our being citizens of heaven doesn't exempt us from pain in this life—only in the next. We all have one choice to make: Each of us can suffer with Christ or without Him. And if the fellowship of citizens of heaven is functioning as God intends it to, no fellow citizen will suffer for long in the solitary company of God.

Before we can understand more thoroughly the fellowship of suffering we have with fellow citizens of heaven, we need to understand some of Christ's pain. What did Paul mean by saying he wanted to share in Christ's suffering?

In any of its forms—physical, emotional, spiritual, mental—suffering may seem hard for some of us to understand. It's one of those concepts so large and vague that it floats over us like a cloud we can't grasp.

It's clear the Lord Jesus emotionally felt the pain of people around Him. He joined with them in a fellowship of suffering.

In looking forward to the day when Jesus would walk the earth, the Old Testament prophet Isaiah said He would be "a man of sorrows [or pains] arid acquainted with grief [or sickness]" (53:3, RSV); one who "has borne our griefs [or sicknesses] and carried our sorrows [or pains]" (53:4, RSV).

It's virtually impossible to separate Jesus' healing ministry from a "fellowship of suffering." Jesus, God Himself made human; certainly had the power to stand on the Mount of Olives or on the temple steps and pronounce healing of anyone within and beyond shouting distance. But no—time after time, He had personal conversations with and even touched the people He healed.

In those days lepers were an especially "unclean" lot, abandoned by their families, thrown out of their homes, left to beg their own bread and live with their own kind. Touching a leper was such a violation of the customs of the day that lepers were obligated to cry out, "Unclean! Unclean!" when they walked down the street. This served as a warning against contamination, ceremonially and spiritually as much as physically. Luke 17:12 describes what was no doubt a typical scene: Jesus entered a village and "was met by 10 lepers, who stood at a distance." They knew they weren't to get too close.

Yet Matthew relates an incredible interaction between Jesus and such an "unclean" man: "Behold, a leper came to him and knelt before him saying, 'Lord, if you will, you can make me clean.' And he stretched out his hand and touched him, saying, 'I will; be clean'" (8:2, 3, RSV). The risk of that touch speaks volumes to me. It's the foundation of a fellowship of suffering.

If Jesus had employed an advertising consultant, He might have beat Ma Bell to her slogan: Reach out and touch someone. After all, that should be the church's motto, not the phone company's.

Jesus saw needs and met them, and as citizens of His kingdom we are called to take on His mind. The compassion that causes Him to reach out to meet needs should prompt us to reach out; the sorrow that causes Him pain should stimulate our own sensitivities.

In our culture I see groups of people we wouldn't dare call "unclean," yet we nevertheless shun them. Take, for instance, the unemployed. When people lose their jobs in America they become social "lepers." People who once worked for them, who curried favor with them, don't find the time to return phone calls. Even the friends they've made outside the workplace tend to step back. Maybe the friend's security is threatened; if lightning struck you, it could strike me. Maybe his respect erodes; if you'd played your cards right, this wouldn't have happened to you; couldn't you see the writing on the wall?

Sometimes such "leprosy" afflicts those who are divorced or widowed. The awareness of our own vulnerability (Could I be the next one who's deserted?) builds a wall that separates friends. Distrust is projected onto old cohorts: Will she make a play for my husband?

A recent article in *Today's Christian Woman* briefly told the story of a new widow who'd looked to her church for comfort and support. But there she'd found instead a tight group of wives who'd excluded her and said, "You're no longer one of us." That woman left the church—any church—and is it a wonder why?

Where was the healing touch, the listening ear, the nourishment? Whatever had become of the fellowship of suffering that Paul saw in the Philippian church? When Paul had been down and put, they'd stuck by him.

But I don't want to give only a negative example. Let me tell you about some incredible people in my church. One woman, whose own personal needs are overwhelming, takes in and cares for foster children. Her powerful, loving influence on those young and not-so-young lives is transforming. Sunday after Sunday I see them, sitting all lined up in a row across the church.

At one time,. for one reason or another, there were two windows broken out of her house. And what happened? Another woman in the congregation came up to me and said, "I've made arrangements to have those windows replaced." Now I knew about the broken windows, but I didn't know that the fuel tank was empty for lack of money. On that count I was totally surprised when another parishioner called—a woman who was ill and struggling for her very life—to tell me that a check was in the mail. to pay for fuel oil for this family. I hadn't solicited either of these responses to need but the fellowship of suffering citizens of heaven, temporarily residing in suburban Pittsburgh, came through on that family's behalf.

Why do some people "come through" so often? Because they see themselves as a part of a fellowship of servants, ready to respond to and obey their Master-King, Jesus Christ. The word *servant* appears several times in Paul's Philippian letter, most notably in chapter two where Paul says, "Your attitude should be the same as that of Christ Jesus." Then Paul goes on to describe characteristics of Jesus' life as a servant.

The Creator took on the nature of a servant, laid aside the prerogative of His sovereignty and took on our human nature. He even died as a condemned man.

Sadly enough, we Christians tend to romanticize the cross. Women wear jeweled crosses around their necks; elaborate gold crosses grace our church altars. But the cross is really a grotesque method of criminal execution. It's as if women wore miniature hangman's nooses around their necks or we set electric chair replicas on our altars.

John provides a telling first-hand account of Jesus the servant, who insisted, that He would wash the feet of His twelve apostles as they gathered for the Passover holiday supper. As you might imagine, washing the guests' dust-covered feet was the job of the most lowly person on hand, a person whose ego was at the low end of the scale—a servant.

John includes an interesting exchange between Jesus and Peter, who refused to allow Jesus to wash his feet. Peter said, "'Lord, do you wash my feet?' Jesus answered him, 'What I am doing you do not know now, but afterward you will understand.' Peter said to him, 'You shall never wash my feet'" (John 13:6–8, RSV).

Then Peter changed his mind and let Jesus serve him. At the end of the scene Jesus explained why He wanted to wash their feet. He said,

"'Do you know what I have done to you? You call me Teacher and Lord; and you are right, for so I am. If I then, your Lord and Teacher, have washed your feet, you also ought to wash one another's feet. For I have given you an example, that you also should do as I have done to you. Truly, truly, I say to you, a servant is not greater than his master; nor is he who is sent greater than he who sent him'" (vv. 12–16, RSV).

Jesus wanted His disciples to follow His example: They were to honor each other and lift one another up by serving. More than that, He wanted them to know that He wasn't asking them to do something that He wasn't Himself willing to do.

Paul wasn't present at the Last Supper, but Jesus' call to servanthood had obviously been well communicated to him. His letters to the church in Rome and Philippi start with salutations in which he refers to himself as a servant of Jesus. In I Corinthians 9:19 Paul refers to himself as a servant of his fellow earth travelers:

"For though I am free from all men, I have made myself a slave to all, that I might win the more." Then, as I've pointed out, Paul passes on to his readers Jesus' call to servanthood as he introduces a description of Jesus' life: "Your attitude should be the same as that of Christ Jesus." In Philippians 3:17 Paul also asks that his readers "join in imitating" himself—the servant.

The Philippians were already well-acquainted with the meaning of servanthood. The word isn't used to describe Epaphroditus, the man who'd left his home in Philippi to minister to Paul in prison, but everything said about him points to a servant-style figure: "fellow worker"; "fellow soldier"; "messenger ...minister to my need"; "risking his life to complete your service to me" (2:25–

30, RSV). Wedged in the middle of these descriptions of Epaphroditus is a command of Paul: "Honor such men."

Most of us resist being servants. It's a dirty word in that we don't want to be slaves. We don't want to be treated ignobly. Servants are the "go-fors" who run around behind the scenes, making other people's lives more pleasant, other people's ministries more powerful. Most of us want to be the up-front person; we want the dignity of office; we want people to take notice of us.

We also want to be totally in control of our schedules. A servant doesn't have the option of telling the master that he just isn't available right now. I expect that Epaphroditus's availability was more useful to God than his ability; that's what servanthood is all about.

Several years ago a friend and I were walking the floor of the annual convention for religious broadcasters held in a Washington, D.C., hotel. Many of the booths are sponsored by companies selling technical equipment to radio stations. Still others feature syndicated ministries, trying to sell their radio or TV program to local station managers.

You can't attend this convention for too long before noticing that it's crawling with religious celebrities presenting a bright, successful image of their work. So after walking up and down a few aisles my friend turned to me and said, "I would guess that there is more ego per square inch in this building right now than anywhere else in the world."

Being horrified at the thought and not wanting to believe that he might be right, I ventured, "The United States Senate might be just as bad." But once he'd said the words, I couldn't get the indictment out of my mind.

Now let me contrast that analysis of our culture with Philip-

pians 2:3.4 RSV: "Do nothing from selfishness or conceit, but in humility count others better than yourselves. Let each of you look not only to his own interests, but also to the interests of others." And from there Paul goes right into the description of Jesus as the epitome of servanthood.

Nobody is asking anybody to play games and imagine that he or she is the most inferior among us. It's not a matter of "I am nothing and you are everything." The idea is that we're to reach out to meet the emotional and physical needs of others— with motives that aren't self-centered and full of conceit.

As Christians we're not to do our good works in the way many corporate foundations give grants. They love to display in glossy brochures how much they give away. and where it's given, because it's all a part of their public relations campaign. They want clients and consumers to think well of them and so they're tax-deductibly generous. No, we're not to do what we do for others so it will look good for ourselves. We're to be a team, always ready to work for the victory of the group and the sponsor rather than for ourselves.

Of course, Jesus Christ is the one and only redeemer of human souls. But on another level, as we Christians imitate Christ's servant style, we can redeem the dignity of those around us. Through an attitude of humility that says to other people, "You are worthy of my respect and encouragement and service," we can in some small way redeem them.

If Jesus could lay aside His godly prerogatives, so much more legitimate than ours, why can't we do it for one another?

—John Guest, born in Oxford, England, is a retired pastor and rector of two Episcopal churches in the U.S. Dr. Guest has authored many books on the Christian life-

style. In addition, his Sunday morning messages have been broadcast on the WORD FM, "LifeFOCUS with John Guest" radio ministry for a number of years.

Reprinted by permission: Charisma Magazine and Strang Communications Company.

October, 1988 Charisma

LESSON 5

MAIN PRINCIPLE

People with the teaching motive gift perform the function of the mind for the body of Christ, while exhorters act as the mouth.

USING OUR GIFTS

by Charlotte Kinvig Bates

THIS ARTICLE IS ONE OF A SERIES EXAMINING THE BASIC TRUTHS OF OUR CHRISTIAN FAITH. AS YOU READ THIS ARTICLE ON "WHY I BELIEVE THAT GOD WANTS ME TO USE THE TALENTS AND GIFTS THAT HE HAS GIVEN TO ME," FOCUS ON HOW THE THOUGHTS PRESENTED CAN DRAW YOU CLOSER TO GOD AND HELP YOU TO LIVE EACH DAY FOR HIM.—ED.

For a number of years I was privileged to play in a brass ensemble that ministered throughout Canada and the United States.

As a member of that team, I was expected to give myself wholeheartedly to that ministry. Simply holding the instrument in my hands and knowing how to play it were not adequate; active participation was what the director required.

Just as the band director expected my full involvement, so I believe that God wants me to develop and to use the talents and gifts that he has given to me. God did not intend that we be spectators. He created each of us for a purpose. God gives us certain abilities with which to serve, but when we become his new creation through salvation in Jesus Christ, he gives us at least one special capacity through which to minister to other people.

In the New Testament these special capacities of gifts refer to divine skills and abilities given through the Holy Spirit to every believer for service to Christ's Church. A clear distinction is made between the *fruit* of the Spirit, which relates to character,[1] and the *gifts*, which pertain to ministry.

THE NATURE OF SPIRITUAL GIFTS

J. I. Packer wrote, "Our exercise of spiritual gifts is nothing more nor less than Christ himself ministering through his Body to his Body, to the Father, and to all people."[2]

Spiritual gifts transcend human capacities. The Holy Spirit may or may not choose to build on our created potential or acquired abilities for the exercise of God-given gifts.

Every believer receives at least one gift for the equipping of the Christian community.[3] Spiritual gifts are not to be used in a selfish or a self-exalting manner.[4]

They are not given for an emotional "high" or for the sake of the spectacular.

Gifts are given and developed in the context of community.

"SPIRITUAL GIFTS ARE NOT TO BE USED IN A SELFISH OR A SELF EXALTING MANNER. THEY ARE NOT GIVEN FOR AN EMOTIONAL 'HIGH' OR FOR THE SAKE OF THE SPECTACULAR"

These gifts vary from one believer to another and are given to complement each other so that the various ministries of the Church can be accomplished. The emphasis of Scripture is biblical unity with diversity.[5]

THE BODY

God's Word uses the metaphor of the human body to help us understand the concept of gifts.[6] The body is one, but it has many parts functioning for the good of the whole.

Chaos would result if the liver would try to do the work of the heart, or the arm to fulfill the work of the brain. Each part of our bodies, and likewise each member of the believing community, needs to exercise the gifts given to ensure the proper functioning of our bodies and of the church.

RESPONSIBILITY

The lack of a particular gift does not mean the removal of Christian responsibility in that area. We may not have the gift of evangelism, but we are still to tell others of our faith in Christ so that they too come to know the Lord Jesus. We may not have the gift of helps, but we are still to assist those in need. Our gifts are not to be used as excuses for failing to fulfill expectations laid out by God for every child of his.

MATURITY

The demonstration of a spiritual gift is not in itself an evidence of spiritual maturity or of godliness. The Church at Corinth is an example of a group of believers who demonstrated various gifts, but who misused the gifts because they lacked spiritual maturity. The Apostle Paul challenged them to "grow up"[7] in Christ and not to use the possession of gifts as the criterion for judging godliness of life and true spirituality.

Our gifts do not define our value as persons. We should not conclude that someone who is given a gift to a greater degree, or a more public gift, is worth more than another person.

DISTRIBUTION OF GIFTS

God is sovereign in his distribution of the various gifts.[8] He gives according to his purpose and his wisdom. Paul encouraged believers to seek those gifts that most contribute to the building up of the Body of Christ: "Eagerly desire the greater gifts." [9]

Theologian D. A. Carson made clear, however, that "Christians may pursue what is best of the [gifts]; but they have no right to any particular one, and ultimately trust the wisdom of their heavenly Father's gracious distribution through the mediation of his Holy Spirit."[10]

> "WE NEED TO DEEPEN OUR COMMITMENT TO BE WISE STEWARDS OF THE GIFTS THAT THE HOLY SPIRIT HAS GIVEN"

These gifts are for all of the people of God; both women and men are gifted by God for the good of others. This is not something in which we boast. Rather, we need to recognize the stewardship which we are called to exercise as a result. This is a way in which the Lord by his Spirit enables us to contribute to the Body.

Possessing and using God's gifts involves:

- *A redeemed relationship.* Apart from entering into salvation, we cannot know that special enabling of the Holy Spirit.
- *A recognition of the divine origin.* God appoints the gifts to each of his children.[11]
- *A church commitment.* As children of God, we need to be active participants within the Body of believers. This not only provides an opportunity for ministry, but also allows for the fellowship that increases effectiveness.
- *A community affirmation.* Recognizing one's spiritual gift is not merely a personal matter. God intends that gifts be clarified, strengthened and affirmed within the context of the Body of Christ.
- *A wise stewardship.* Possession of a gift or gifts means facing divine accountability. We are responsible to God for what he has entrusted to us. Proper investment is related to eternal reward.
- *Loving service.* While we are convinced that God wants us to use the gifts that he has given to us, we need to recognize that if they are not exercised in love for those to whom we are ministering, they accomplish nothing.[12]

We have been redeemed by Christ Jesus to worship and glorify God as well as to serve him forever. Therefore, we need to deepen our commitment to be wise stewards of the gifts that the Holy Spirit has given, seeking to live out Christ's love and holiness in ways that will glorify God.

(1) Galatians 5:16–26. (2) From "Keep in Step With the Spirit," by J. I. Packer, @1984 J. I. Packer, Fleming H. Revell Company, Baker Book House Company, Grand Rapids, Michigan. (3) 1 Corinthians 12:7; Ephesians 4:11–12. (4) Romans 12:3. (5) 1 Corinthians 12:1–31. (6) Ephesians 4:15–16. (7) Ephesians 4:15, KJV. (8) Ephesians 4:7. (9) 1 Corinthians 12:31, NIV. (10) From "Showing the Spirit: A Theological Exposition of 1 Corinthians 12–14," by D. A. Carson, ©1987 Baker Book House Company, Grand Rapids, Michigan. (11) 1 Corinthians 12:28. (12) 1 Corinthians 13:1–3; 14:1. The Bible verse marked NIV is taken by permission from The Holy Bible, New International Version, copyright ©1973, 1978, 1984 International Bible Society, Colorado Springs, Colorado

—Charlotte Kinvig Bates has served as the Dean of Prairie Graduate School in Calgary, Alberta, as well as chair of the board of directors of Women Alive of Canada, and a member of the executive board of the International Centre for Ministry Development.

Reprinted by permission: BGEA ©1994 Billy Graham Evangelistic Association.

LESSON 6

MAIN PRINCIPLE

People with a giving motive gift perform the function of extended arms, while people with the gift of administration serve as the shoulders of the body of Christ.

SEEKING MORE OF THE SPIRIT

by Mike Bickle

In a nation saturated with the proclamation of the gospel, what often is lacking is the *demonstration* of the gospel. Paul said, "Our gospel came to you not simply with words, but also with power, with the Holy Spirit and with deep conviction" (1 Thess. 1:5, NIV).

To be effective in fulfilling Christ's commission, I believe we must earnestly desire to see the gifts of the Spirit manifested in our lives. The first step is to receive a greater measure of the Holy Spirit.

The Word says the Holy Spirit was with you even before salvation, convicting you of "sin and righteousness and judgment" (John 16:8). When you first accepted Christ, you received the Holy Spirit living in you (John 14:16–18). You began to experience the fruit of the Spirit; that is, your character began to change. But Jesus and His followers illustrate that more than good character is needed to fully demonstrate the gospel.

The Word also speaks of a dynamic encounter with the Holy Spirit that empowers believers for ministry. Jesus said, "You shall receive power when the Holy Spirit comes on you" (Acts 1:8), a promise fulfilled as believers were "filled with the Holy Spirit" (Acts 2:4; 4:31; 13:52).

Pentecostals and charismatics typically refer to the initial experi-

> I IMAGINE GOD ALMOST STRAINING IN HIS EAGERNESS TO RELEASE MORE OF THE HOLY SPIRIT THROUGH OUR LIVES.

ence of the Spirit's fullness as being "baptized with the Holy Spirit" (Luke 3:16; Acts 1:5). But by whatever term it is called, such an encounter is the gateway into a new dimension of the Spirit's presence and power. If you've never experienced an extra measure of the Holy Spirit, know that God is eager for you to have the full measure of His presence in your life. Confess any sin and surrender to the lordship of Christ. Tell the Lord that you long for a closer, more intimate life with Him. Begin to worship the Lamb. You may want to close your eyes, lift your hands or sing quietly. Enter His presence and wait before Him in faith.

What should you expect to happen? While I personally reject the dogmatic insistence that speaking in tongues is the only true evidence of being filled or baptized with the Holy Spirit, I do believe it is the New

Testament norm. "*All* of them were filled with the Holy Spirit and began to speak in other tongues" (Acts 2:4, emphasis mine). I encourage you to expect it to happen to you, too.

Another spiritual principle comes into play at this point. The Bible teaches us not to despise the day of small beginnings and to be faithful with little before we're entrusted with much. While I've seen many people literally burst forth with an entire vocabulary in their personal prayer language, I've also seen people follow the natural order: starting small and growing.

This was true for me personally. I experienced tongues with only a syllable or two at first. But through faithfulness, my personal prayer language grew.

As you pray, you may also experience any number of other phenomena. Some people laugh, others weep. You may feel warm all over. Many people sense a stillness and inner peace that is different from anything they've ever experienced. You may find yourself singing, worshiping or prophesying. The important thing, however, is not the externals, but the internals. I believe that if you are born again of the Spirit and you ask our heavenly Father to release His gifts through you, He will be faithful (Luke 11:13).

November 1992, Charisma

I often imagine God leaning forward, almost straining in His eagerness to release more of the Spirit through our lives. One of the Spirit's roles is to glorify Jesus.. "He (the Holy Spirit) will bring glory to me," Jesus said (John 16:14). The Father is passionate for His Son. He is committed to seeing every knee bow before Jesus. Because the Holy Spirit glorifies Jesus, the Father is eager to grant Him in greater measure. But He will not force Himself on us. If we have not, it's because we have not asked. When we ask Him to pour out His Spirit upon us, He is ready, willing and able.

After inviting the Holy Spirit to rest upon you in power, you will see the gifts of the Spirit operate through you. Almost no one suddenly begins raising the dead and emptying the hospitals. But you can expect to be used. Initially your job is making yourself available. God may give you knowledge, wisdom, healing or even a miracle for someone—but you have to be available.

The Christian life is relational. Jesus was involved in the lives of others—both believers and non-believers. If you're not involved in a small group, consider getting involved. In my experience, small groups often provide an ideal setting for beginning to release spiritual gifts. You'll have plenty of opportunities to hear the needs of others, pray for their sicknesses and offer encouragement.

Allow the compassion of God to flow through you, and ask Him to use you in whatever way He sees fit.

—Mike Bickle is an author and the director of the International House of Prayer Missions Base of Kansas City (IHOP–KC), an organization based on 24/7 prayer with worship that is engaged in inner city outreaches along with justice initiatives, planting houses of prayer, and training missionaries.

Reprinted by permission: Charisma Magazine and Strang Communications Company.

November 1992, Charisma

THE GIFTS, THE CALLING AND THE ANOINTING

by John Stocker

THE GIFTS

The Amplified Bible translates Romans 11:29: "For God's gifts and His call are irrevocable—He never withdraws them when once they are given, and He does not change His mind about those to whom He gives His grace or to whom He sends His call." Before we were born, God gave us abilities and gifts. He will never take those from us.

Many people today despise the gifts God has placed in their lives. The one who has an ability to work with children wants to work with teens. The one who works with teens wants to pastor the church. The Sunday School teacher wants to be the deacon. The deacon wants to be the usher. Many try to do things for which God hasn't gifted them, and they want Him to anoint them in those areas. But the gift and the anointing go hand in hand. God does not anoint what He has not gifted. And there is a difference between the gifts and the anointing.

But we can choose to trust the Father, accepting with an open heart those abilities He has distributed to us, and develop them. Then we will become able ministers in the areas in which God has equipped us.

Only then will we find fulfillment.

THE CALLING

Paul says that the gifts and the calling of God are irrevocable. Since the word "calling" is singular, it must refer to the general calling that comes to every born-again Christian. All born-again believers are "the called." Romans 8:28 says, "... We know that all things work together for good to them that love God, to them who are the called according to his purpose." Every Christian has been "called out of darkness into his marvelous light" (1 Pet. 2:9). We're all called to be His witnesses, to heal the sick, to cast out devils, to bind up the brokenhearted, to be salt and light, to destroy the works of the devil.

If people would stop worrying about receiving a specific call, and start doing the things all Christians have been called to do, they would automatically flow into their individual calling. The Word tells us, "...As God hath distributed to every man, as the Lord hath called every one, so let him walk..." (I Cor. 7:17). Every man, woman and child in the kingdom of God has a divine appointment. When God puts His hand on somebody's life and directs him in His calling—whether it is to be a doctor or a lawyer, a pastor or an evangelist—He will so do in accordance with the gifts He distributed to that person. He calls us to use our gifts for the kingdom of God. People who refuse to develop their God-given talents will be frustrated. They can't understand why the anointing of God does not rest on their lives.

There are two erroneous ideas concerning the calling of God. The first is the elitist view: only a few people are called. Everybody else should just sit in the pew. How worthless is the Christian who doesn't feel called of God! He has no vision, no drive, no motivation; he simply exists. Our churches are filled with this kind of Christian today: Christian who do not realize that whether they are doctors, iron workers, or construction workers—they are called of God to be salt and light where they are. That's why some churches don't grow.

The second fallacy regarding the calling of God is that just because a person wants to do something for God, he is called. We can spend a lifetime failing to recognize and give God glory for what He has distributed to us. If we determine to do something we were never equipped to do, we will be defeated, frustrated and angry.

THE ANOINTING

Every believer has been anointed with the Holy Spirit. But special anointings of the Holy Spirit come upon believers for service in the kingdom of God. Ministry is worthless without the anointing. The anointing of the Holy Spirit changes us, lifting us out of ourselves and bringing us into the realm of the supernatural. It also changes those to whom we minister, bringing life and ushering them into the realm of the heavenlies.

How does God decide whom He's going to anoint? I Samuel 16 contains the account of Samuel's search for King Saul's successor. Initially, Samuel believed he had found the man when he saw Jesse's oldest son, Eliab. Samuel looked on Eliab's outward appearance and said, "Surely the Lord's anointed is before him. But the Lord said unto Samuel, Look not on his countenance, or on the height of his stature; because I have refused him: for the Lord seeth not as man seeth; *for man looketh on the outward appearance, but the Lord looketh on the heart*" (I Sam. 16:6, 7). God looks for a pure heart upon which He can pour the anointing. It was not Eliab, but David whom God had chosen as Saul's successor.

This is a good illustration of what frequently happens in the body of Christ. Often believers look at someone's talent, ability or charisma and confuse those things with God's anointing. So much in the Church today is entertainment. Entertainment cannot take you into the presence of the Lord, nor can it change hearts. Only the anointing can do these things. We, as believers, must learn to look beyond talent and the ability to entertain. We must ask ourselves one question: If Jesus had been ministering, would He have ministered the same things, in the same spirit and in the same way?

If a person's heart is not right, God still loves him, but He refuses to put His anointing upon that individual's life. The Bible says, "The heart is deceitful above all things, and desperately wicked: who can know it?" (Jer. 17:9). The wickedness of the heart is the number one problem in receiving and keeping God's anointing. We must ask God daily to prune our hearts, to circumcise them by the power of the Holy Ghost. "Keep thy heart with all diligence; for out of it are the issues of life" (Prov. 4:23). We must commit ourselves to a lifetime of seeking God.

The Bible contains many examples of people who had the anointing of the Holy Spirit and lost it. The most obvious one would be Satan: "Thou art the anointed cherub that covereth; and I have set thee so...." But he lost that anointing. The reason? "Thine heart was lifted up because of thy beauty, thou hast corrupted thy wisdom by reason of thy brightness: I will cast thee to the ground, I will lay thee before kings that they may behold thee" (Ezek. 28:14,17). Satan was probably the most anointed creature in the universe, but he lost that anointing because of pride—the number one killer of all anointing.

We sometimes do not seek God for His anointing because our hearts are filled with pride over the talents and abilities God has given us. But talent, ability, charisma, good looks—even if a person has them all—cannot compare with the life-changing power of God's anointing.

A classic example of a man of God who lost the anointing is Samson. Samson played with sin. Like Samson, many anointed men and women believe they're always going to have the anointing—regardless of how they live. Nothing could be further from the truth!

The anointing remains only upon those who have a pure heart, those who have a heart after God, those whose motives are right.

Remember Peter's response to Simon the Sorcerer, who wanted to buy the power of God: "Thou hast neither part nor lot in this matter: for thy heart is not right in the sight of God" (Acts 8:21). God's anointing was not available to him because his heart was not right.

Having a pure heart does not mean being sinless. The Bible says, "If we say that we have no sin, we deceive ourselves, and the truth is not in us" (I Jn.1:8). Sometimes we think we have no sin because we compare ourselves with someone other than the One in whose image we were made. As we look at Him, we will quickly realize that we have all "...come short of the glory of God" (Rom.3:23). We will always have shortcomings we're working on.

David exemplifies a man with a pure heart. And yet we also know of the terrible sin David committed. But David, who had previously experienced the fellowship with God that a pure heart brings, cried out to God in remorse and anguish when he realized what he had done. This man of God freely admitted his sin, and pleaded with God "...Take not Thy Holy Spirit from me" (Ps.51:11). He recognized his need for the anointing of God's Spirit.

If we lose the anointing, can we get it back? Of course; we simply go to the Lord openly and honestly, allowing Him to cleanse our hearts. His anointing rests on us as long as our hearts are after Him, our motives are right and pure, and we're seeking Him daily to cleanse our hearts. God is rich in mercy. We are not worthy of His anointing, but those to whom we're ministering need Him.

A pure heart is not the only requirement for receiving the anointing of God. We must also go and do that which God tells us to do. God did not call us to sit around, enjoying His presence. He called us to touch our world in these last days with the power of the Holy Ghost.

—Adapted from a message given at Christ For The Nations in Dallas, TX.

John Stocker is the former Senior Pastor of Resurrection Fellowship in Loveland, Colorado.

Reprinted by permission: Christ for the Nations, CFNI, P.O. Box 769000, Dallas, TX 75376-9000, 800-933-2364.

LESSON 7

MAIN PRINCIPLE

*People with the compassion motive gift perform the function
of the heart of the body of Christ. Each of the motive gifts
reveals to the world a different aspect of God's character.
When we understand each other and the way God made us,
we can complete each other, not compete with each other.*

MOTIVE GIFTS COMPARISON

1. Perception
  a. Declares truth and insight. Perceives where people or programs really are in light of God's Word.
  b. Has the motivation to reveal unrighteous motives or actions by presenting God's truth. Wants to make motives right.
  c. Meets spiritual needs.

2. Serving
  a. Provides practical assistance and help. Sees what needs to be done and does it.
  b. Has the motivation to demonstrate love by meeting practical needs and by rendering assistance.
  c. Meets practical needs.

3. Teaching
  a. Clarifies truth and doctrine.
  b. Has the motivation to search out and validate the truth. Has the ability to impart knowledge and to lead others into revealed truth.
  c. Meets intellectual needs.

4. Exhortation
  a. Gives encouragement.
  b. Has the motivation to stimulate the faith of others. Is able to encourage people to grow and meet successfully the experiences of life.
  c. Meets personal growth needs.

5. Giving
  a. Shares assets and provides material assistance.
  b. Has the motivation to provide for the work of God by enabling the ministry of others to go forward and succeed. Is able to see needs and to give away assets.
  c. Meets financial and material needs.

6. Administration
  a. Organizes and provides leadership aid.
  b. Has the motivation to coordinate the activities of others to achieve common goals. Is able to see long-range goals and to facilitate others in appropriate tasks.
  c. Meets organizational aid and effectiveness needs.

7. Compassion
  a. Provides support and empathy.
  b. Has the motivation to identify with and to relieve those who are in distress. Is able to feel where people are and to identify with their needs.
  c. Meets emotional needs.

FRESH OIL

by Gregg Headley

Oil is a symbol of the Holy Spirit. Samuel anointed David to be king. When he took over the throne of Israel, David purposed in his heart to honor God.

In his tremendous prayer of repentance, David prayed, "Do not take Your Holy Spirit from me" (Psa. 51:11). He knew that if he was going to lead the nation of Israel, it could only happen as a result of the Spirit of God resting upon his life, providing the anointing necessary for leadership.

In Psalm 92:8–10 David made this confession of faith: "But You, LORD, are on high forevermore. For behold, Your enemies, O LORD, for behold, Your enemies shall perish; all the workers of iniquity shall be scattered. But my horn You have exalted like a wild ox; I have been anointed with fresh oil."

God gave Moses very specific instructions on how worship was to be conducted in the tabernacle, including how to make and utilize the holy anointing oil. "And you shall make from these a holy anointing oil, an ointment compounded according to the art of the perfumer. It shall be a holy anointing oil" (Ex. 30:25). God gave detailed orders regarding the contents of that holy anointing oil and how it was to be used. "It shall not be poured on man's flesh; nor shall you make any other like it,

according to its composition. It is holy, and it shall be holy to you" (Ex. 30:32). This holy anointing oil is a type of the New Testament anointing with the power of God's Holy Spirit.

The anointing of God cannot be reproduced by human intellect, ingenuity, talent or energy. The anointing comes only by the Spirit of God being poured out on us: There is no substitute for the power of the Holy Spirit. Nothing else can enable us to fulfill the plan and the purpose of God in our lives.

When we think about the condition of our world today—the events that are taking place in the Middle East, what's happening in America's society—the enemy is having a heyday. There are tremendous forces at work to try to destroy this world. But God has said in His word that "it shall come to pass in the last days ... I will pour out of My Spirit on all flesh" (Acts 2:17).

Even though there is great wickedness and turmoil these days, there is also a great move of God beginning to take place around this world. There's going to be a mighty outpouring and move of God's Spirit before He comes again. The words of Zechariah are still true: "'Not by might nor by power, but by My Spirit,' says the LORD of hosts." (Zech. 4:6).

The indispensable element

necessary to accomplish great things for God is the power and the anointing of the Holy Spirit. Exodus 30:26–29 says, "With it you shall anoint the tabernacle of meeting and the ark of the Testimony (which contained the Ten Commandments, the Word of God, the will of God); the table and all its utensils, the lampstand and its utensils, and the altar of incense; the altar of burnt offering with all its utensils, and the laver and its base. You shall sanctify them, that they may be most holy."

God was teaching a very important lesson here: Every function of ministry, every article and building used in ministry and all the furnishings in those buildings need to have the touch of God upon them. Every aspect and article of worship—the piano, the podium, the musical instruments—needs to have the touch of God upon it because the worship facility has been set apart, sanctified for the purpose of God. We need to treat it accordingly, recognizing it as such.

"And you shall anoint Aaron and his sons, and sanctify them, that they may minister to Me as priests" (Ex. 30:30). Aaron was not qualified for ministry until he had the touch of God upon his life. Aaron and his sons were not qualified to fulfill the function of the priesthood until they had been anointed.

Your ministry will not come because you've been given an office somewhere, been given a title or because someone has signed a paper saying you're licensed or ordained. Those things cannot produce ministry. The only way effective ministry will take place is by the anointing and the power of the Holy Spirit.

The supreme example in the New Testament Who indicated our need for the work of the Holy Spirit in our lives was none other than Jesus Christ. He was the One Who stood out above all others, demonstrating the work of the Spirit of God in His life. Every facet of His ministry was accomplished as a result of that.

The angel spoke to Mary, "The Holy Spirit will come upon you. and the power of the Highest will overshadow you; therefore also, that Holy One who is to be born will be called the Son of God" (Lk.1:35). The miraculous birth of Jesus took place by the power of the Holy Spirit. Jesus was born of the Spirit into this world.

When Jesus was baptized, "the Holy Spirit descended in bodily form like a dove upon Him" (Lk. 3:22). "Then Jesus, being filled with the Holy Spirit, returned from the Jordan and was led by the Spirit into the wilderness" (Lk.4:1).

Jesus was born of the Spirit, He was filled with the Spirit and the Spirit *led* Jesus in His life. When Jesus was tempted by Satan, He came out victorious. "Then Jesus returned (this is after His temptation) in the *power* of the Spirit to Galilee" (Lk.4:14).

Jesus then went to His hometown of Nazareth and read from the scroll in the synagogue. "The Spirit of the LORD is upon Me, because He has *anointed* Me to preach the gospel to the poor. He has sent Me to heal the brokenhearted, to preach deliverance to the captives and recovery of sight to the blind, to set at liberty those who are oppressed, to preach the acceptable year of the LORD"

(Lk.4:18,19). Everything Jesus did in His ministry is contained in those two verses. How did it happen? By the anointing of the Spirit.

When Jesus submitted Himself to the will of the Father and made His way to the cross as a sacrifice, it was through the power of the Holy Spirit: "Christ, who through the eternal Spirit offered Himself without spot to God" (Heb.9:14).

Every aspect of the life and the ministry of Jesus Christ was accomplished by virtue of the work of the Holy Spirit. He was born of the Spirit. He was led of the Spirit. He was filled with the Spirit. Scripture says He was full of the Spirit without measure. He was anointed by the Spirit to fulfill all of His earthly ministry (Lk.4:18).

It was the Spirit of God that raised Christ from the dead. Paul says that the same Spirit that raised Christ from the dead dwells in you and me. That Spirit can quicken or give life to our mortal bodies (Rom.8:11).

Jesus Christ; the very Son of the living God, when He came to this earth and became flesh, needed the Holy Spirit of God to accomplish His purpose. Why do ministers often think that some program, organizational system, music or the "right" team is going to get the job done? Those things have their place, but if they don't have the anointing of God upon them, the job won't be done.

On the other hand, a man or a woman may not have all the tools of ministry or the ability to give a tremendous oration, but with the power of the Holy Spirit in their lives, nothing can stop him or her. Because the same Spirit that raised Christ from the dead also lives in them.

In fact, Jesus told His disciples. "Tarry in the city of Jerusalem until you are endued with power from on high" (Lk.24:49). He had already instructed them that God would give the Holy Spirit to those who ask. He said "If anyone thirsts,

let him come to Me and drink. Out of his heart will flow rivers of living water" (Jn.7:37,38).

There are two kinds of wells. With one you have to put the bucket down, turn the crank, draw the water and then you're refreshed. But then there's the artesian well that you have to put a cap on because it flows and flows. Many people are doing ministry in the kind of well where a lot of effort must be put forth to bring limited results. But God wants His Church to tap into the artesian well of His Spirit. That way, ministry pours forth out of the heart.

Some people in the Church equate the anointing with how loud you preach and how much energy you expend. But some of the most anointed men of God haven't had to yell to prove it. It was evident because of the work of God that took place. Do you ever remember Jesus sweating to get the work done? No. The anointing just flowed, and as a result, the work was accomplished.

When it comes to worship and ministry, you and I need a fresh touch of God. To defeat the enemy, it will take a fresh touch of God upon your life. If you're going into battle, you must have God's anointing. II Samuel 1:21 says, "The shield of Saul, not anointed with oil." Saul went out to battle without the blessing of God upon him because he was no longer walking in the anointing.

We do not wrestle against flesh and blood. Our warfare is spiritual. Our weapons of warfare are not carnal, but they are mighty through God to pull down strongholds. But do not underestimate the power of darkness to defeat you if you are walking in the arm of the flesh. If your shield is not anointed, you're in trouble. You and I have to depend upon God every single time we attempt to minister in any form or fashion if anything is going to be accomplished.

Every child of God needs

the power of the Holy Spirit. Jesus came to baptize us with the Holy Ghost and with fire so that we would be ministered to, equipped and empowered to be His witness. It won't work to try to operate on an old anointing. You need a fresh touch of God—to be anointed with fresh oil.

— Adapted from a message given at CFNI in Dallas.

Gregg Headley has pastored in Dallas, Texas and ministered throughout Central America, Europe, the South Pacific, and the former Soviet Union. He serves on the boards of Dallas Teen Life Challenge (a national drug rehabilitation program), Dallas Dream Center (an inner-city ministry to children, teens and adults), Commonwealth of Independent States Bible Schools (training center for men and women for roles in the national church), and Mongolian Assemblies of God Bible School).

Reprinted by permission: Christ for the Nations, CFNI, P.O. Box 769000, Dallas, TX 75376-9000, 800-933-2364.

LESSON 8

MAIN PRINCIPLE

An exciting and fulfilling relationship with the Holy Spirit is available to all believers. We are called into a deeper realm of God through daily communion with the Holy Spirit. It is out of a relationship with Him that God will pour out His powerful love on a hurting world.

THE HOLY SPIRIT—WHO IS HE?

A. The Holy Spirit at Creation

"In the beginning..."

1. Acts 17:24 <u>God the Father was present</u>

2. John 1:1–3; Col. 1:16–17 <u>Jesus was present</u>

3. Genesis 1:2–3 <u>The Holy Spirit was present</u>

B. The Holy Spirit in the New Testament

1. He authored the Scriptures.

   2 Peter 1:21

2. In the life of Jesus

   a. Luke 1:35

   b. Luke 2:40

   c. Luke 3:21–22

   d. Luke 4:1, 14

3. Jesus promised the Holy Spirit and taught these truths about Him.

   a. John 14:16–17 <u>Jesus would send the Holy Spirit</u>

   b. John 14:16

   c. John 14:17 _____

   d. John 14:17 _____

   e. John 14:17 _____

   f. John 14:26_____

   g. John 14:26; 15:26_____

   h. John 15:26_____

   i. John 16:8_____

   j. John 16:13_____

   k. John 16:14 _____

4. After His resurrection Jesus again promised the Holy Spirit.

   a. Luke 24:49_____

   b. Acts 1:4, 5, 8_____

5. The Holy Spirit was sent after Jesus ascended into heaven.

   a. Acts 2:1–4_____

   b. Acts 5:32_____

   c. Acts 7:55; 11:24; 19:6 _____

C. The Holy Spirit's Role in our Lives

1. John 14:16 _____

2. John 14:17 _____

3. John 14:26 _____

4. John 16:8 _____

5. John 16:13 _____

6. John 16:14–15 <u>He reveals Christ to us</u> _____

D. The Holy Spirit is a Person! He is to us as Christ was to the disciples.

1. Ephesians 4:30_____

2. Romans 8:27_____

3. Corinthians 12:11 _____

E. The Holy Spirit Brings Christ Glory—John 16:14

1. He is the Spirit of Truth, just as Jesus is the truth (John 14:6).

2. He reminds us of Jesus' words.

3. He is the vehicle that God uses to speak to us the things that are on His heart.

4. He makes us more like Jesus.

5. He brings us into true worship.

6. He desires that we give our praise to Jesus.

Because of Jesus' shed blood at Calvary, we now have direct access into the presence of God the Father. Because of the Holy Spirit, we can walk (Galatians 5:25), talk (John 10:27) and move in the same power (Luke 24:47-49) Jesus had when He walked the earth.

HOW TO DONATE TO ZOE MINISTRIES

Help us deliver the message of Life throughout the World!

In addition to providing support for ZOE missions, curriculum
development/translation and course scholarships, many of our
translated materials will be donated to believers
without resources to purchase them.

Would you prayerfully consider supporting this ministry?

YOU ARE ABLE TO MAKE A DONATION IN ANY OF THE FOLLOWING WAYS:

Online with PayPal Account or Credit Card via PayPal
This gives you a safe and easy way to make
designated contributions.

Visit our website to make a secure online donation.
www.zoeministries.org/donor-partners/

By Automatic Bill Pay
Recurring donations to ZOE or to a designated
ZOE missionary may be set up with your bank.

By Check
Please make checks payable to 'ZOE Ministries International'
Our Address is – PO Box 2207, Arvada CO 80001-2207, USA

May God bless you richly for your support of this ministry!

"Now this is eternal life [zoe]: that they may know you, the only true God, and Jesus Christ, whom you have sent." - John 17:3

LESSON 9

MAIN PRINCIPLE

We need to get to know who the Holy Spirit is and how He works together with the Father and with Jesus. Then we can draw closer to Him and cooperate with Him as He works through us to bring glory to God.

OUTLINE TO ACCOMPANY THE TRINITY TEACHING

I. Introduction
A. Galatians 5:25

B. Psalm 37:23

II. In the Beginning
A. The Trinity Created the Heavens and the Earth—Genesis 1:1–3
1. The Father—Acts 17:24
2. The Son—John 1:1–3; Colossians 1:16–17
3. The Holy Spirit—Genesis 1:2

B. Mankind—God's Special Creation
1. Man's Position—Genesis 1:26, 31; 2:7
2. Man's Fall—Genesis 2:16–17; 3:8–10, 21; 6:5–6

III. God Reveals More of Himself
A. Elohim—Genesis 1:1

B. Jehovah– "I AM WHO I AM"—Exodus 3:14

IV. Jesus, the Lamb
A. The Atoning Sacrifice
Genesis 3:15; John 3:16–18; John 1:29; 1 John 4:9–10; Isaiah 53:7, 12b

B. Jesus' Relationship:
1. With the Father—Matthew 3:16–17; John 5:19, 30; 7:16; 8:28; Mark 14:35–36
2. With the Holy Spirit—Luke 4:1, 14, 18–19; Acts 10:38

V. The Holy Spirit
A. Jesus Taught the Disciples About the Holy Spirit and His Work
John 14:15–26; John 16:7–15; Acts 1:4–5, 8

B. The Impartation of the Holy Spirit
1. Filling the Disciples—Acts 2
2. Symbols of the Holy Spirit—Acts 2:1–4; Matthew 3:16
3. Making Us More Like Jesus—2 Corinthians 3:18
4. Bringing Glory to Jesus the King and God the Father—John 4:23–24; John 14:26; John 16:14; Galatians 4:4–7; Romans 8:15–16

HOW TO HEAR GOD'S VOICE — IN CHRIST

TRINITY DIAGRAM

YHWH
"I AM WHO I AM"
Exodus 3:14

ELOHIM
"GOD THE CREATOR"
Genesis 1:1

ABBA
"FATHER"
Romans 8:15

John 1:29

JESUS, THE LAMB

Revelation 17:14

JESUS, THE KING

Acts 2:3

HOLY SPIRIT

Matthew 3:16

HOLY SPIRIT

John 3:16

THE TRINITY

ROLES OF THE FATHER, SON, AND HOLY SPIRIT

by David L. Jenkins

The concept of the Trinity, God in three Persons, is one of the most profound and important doctrines in the Bible. Yet when early Christian believers began openly to acknowledge Jesus Christ as the Son of God and to recognize the Holy Spirit as the indwelling presence of God, they were accused by many Jews of violating the worship of one God. The basic confession of the Jews concerning God is strictly monotheistic: "Hear, O Israel: The Lord our God, the Lord is one" (Deut.6:4).

Arising against this background, and concentrating more on evangelism and survival than on theology, the early church allowed several centuries to pass before expressing a clear doctrine of the Trinity.

THE TRINITY:

GOD EXISTS AS THREE PERSONS

OF ONE ESSENCE.

A BRIEF HISTORY OF TRINITARIAN DOCTRINE

The crucial turning point for the debate concerning the Trinity came when the Roman emperor Constantine convened a council of the church at the city of Nicaea in A.D. 325. The two main opposing views were held by Arius and Athanasius, both of whom were church officials from Alexandria, Egypt.

Arius maintained that there is only one God who had no beginning, and that the Son was created out of nothing by this eternal God before God made the world. The Son thus became the greatest and first of all created beings, but was different and apart from God the father.

Athanasius contended that the Son is eternally generated by God the Father, and is of the same essence as the Father. Although there is no division in God's essential being, the Son is a distinct Person.

Constantine sided with Athanasius and the Council of Nicaea produced a bedrock statement concerning the Trinity. It begins: "We believe in one God, Father Almighty, maker of all things visible and invisible; and in one Lord Jesus Christ the Son of God, begotten of the Father, only begotten, that is from the substance of the Father."

Near the bottom of its creed, the council added the brief statement, "And (we believe) in the Holy Spirit."

Fifty-six years later, the church's Council of Constantinople stated more fully that the Father, Son, and Holy Spirit constitute one Godhead, existing simultaneously in three modes of being.

HINTS OF THE TRINITY IN THE OLD TESTAMENT

Though the exact wording of the Trinitarian doctrine defined by the councils is not found at any one place in the Bible, the Trinity is a biblical doctrine. It is most clearly seen in the New Testament. But even the Old Testament contains inklings of it.

Some Bible experts have suggested that the triple description of the creation of humans by God in Genesis 1:27 contains a hint of God's Trinity. "God created man in his own image, in the image of God he created him; male and female he created them."

Elohim, the plural Hebrew name for God, is used approximately five hundred times in the first five books of the Bible, followed consistently by a singular verb (see Gen. 1:26, 27; 3:22; 11:7). Many scholars believe that Elohim reveals the oneness of God as well as a plurality of Persons in the Godhead.

There are numerous other Old Testament references to individual members of the Trinity. The Spirit of God is refereed to early in the Book of Genesis (1:2), as well as at other places in the Old Testament. Isaiah 7:14 speaks of Immanuel, "God with us," whom we know to be Jesus, the Son of God. God the Father, the "I" in Psalm 2:7 stated that it was His intention to recognize His Son as the supreme ruler of the earth.

God is distinguished from the Holy Spirit in Psalm 104:30, where God is described as sending forth His Spirit.

NEW TESTAMENT REVELATIONS OF THE TRINITY

Whereas the doctrine of the Trinity is partially concealed in the Old Testament, it is marvelously revealed in the New Testament. The names Father, Son, and Holy Spirit are used both separately and together. Also, all three Persons are declared to be God (John 1:1, 9:54; Acts 5:3, 4). The unity of God is noted in the New Testament (John 17:3; I Cor. 9:4; I Tim. 2:5), along with the teaching that the Godhead consists of three Persons.

Among the Scriptures concerning Jesus' birth, there is unmistakable testimony to the involvement of Father, Son, and Holy Spirit. The angel Gabriel told Mary, "The Holy Spirit will come upon you, and the power of the Most High will overshadow you. So the holy one to be born will be called the Son of God" (Luke 1:35).

When Jesus was baptized and about to begin His ministry; the Holy Spirit descended upon Him, and the Father spoke His approval from heaven (Matt. 3:16, 17). In His preaching, Jesus dwelt not only on His own work, but also on the work of His Father and God and of the Spirit. Jesus boldly claimed to be the Son of God and one empowered by the Holy Spirit (Matt. 12:28; Luke 10:22; 12:12; 22:70).

One of the most remarkable biblical groupings of the three Persons of the Godhead is found in Jesus' teaching concerning the coming of the Holy Spirit. Jesus said, "The Counselor, the Holy Spirit, whom the Father will send in my name, will teach you all things and will remind you of everything I have said to you" (John 14:26).

THE INTERRELATIONSHIP AND ROLES OF THE THREE PERSONS

The Great Commission Jesus gave His disciples may be the nearest approach to a formal presentation of the Trinity in the New Testament. "Go and make disciples of all nations, baptizing them in the name of the Father and of the Son and of the Holy Spirit" (Matt. 28:19). Jesus said that there is only one "name," indicating the unity of the Godhead, and three designations of the one God—Father, Son, and Holy Spirit.

The apostle Paul regularly in his epistles alluded to the Trinity. God the Father, the Lord Jesus Christ, and the Holy Spirit appear in Paul's writings as equal objects of adoration and praise. For instance, Paul pronounced a profound benediction upon his readers at the close of his second letter to the Corinthian believers: "May the grace of the Lord Jesus Christ, and the love of God, and the fellowship of the Holy Spirit be with you all" (II Cor. 13:14).

Paul's Ephesian letter is saturated with references to the Trinity. He clearly stated that the access of Jews and Gentiles to the throne of grace involves the Trinity: "Through [Christ] we both have access to the Father by one Spirit" (Eph. 2:18). Furthermore, Paul emphasized that the resources for the believer's daily walk and spiritual warfare are found in the Trinity (Eph. 5:18–20; 6:10–18).

From the biblical evidence, we can conclude that God the Father is the original source of all things. God the Son, in the process of the Father's manifestation of Himself to the world, came as the embodiment of divine love and grace. The Holy Spirit, the final revelation of God, bestows the blessings of the Father and the Son upon God's children. The Holy Spirit also convicts the world of sin, helps the believer understand God's Word, and seals those who are redeemed by God's grace.

While we will never fully comprehend the mystery and unity of the Trinity, we give equal reverence, love, and obedience to the Father, Son and Holy Spirit.

—Scripture quotations are from the New International Version.

David L. Jenkins is an author and has pastored the First Baptist Church of Gilmer, Texas.

QUENCH NOT THE HOLY SPIRIT

by Vinson Synan

There is a longing in the hearts of most Christians to worship God in spirit and in truth. Learning how to move with and be free in the Holy Spirit concerns your will; you decide whether or not you will worship God in spirit and in truth. God made you a free moral agent.

I Thess. 5:19 says, "Quench not the Spirit." To quench a fire, you *decide* to pour water on the blaze and put it out. To quench the Spirit is to *decide* not to cooperate with the Holy Spirit. Individuals, nations or denominations can either quench the Spirit or move with the Spirit.

There are 5 primary steps to apostasy. *Quenching* the Spirit is the first step. The second step is called *grieving* the Spirit: "And grieve not the Holy Spirit of God, whereby ye are sealed unto the day of redemption" (Eph. 4:30). The Holy Spirit is a person and we can grieve Him until He weeps because of our failure to serve God as we should. The third step is *resisting* the Holy Spirit. Acts 7:51 states, "...ye do always resist the Holy Ghost: as your fathers did, so do ye." The religious leaders of Israel were resisting the Holy Ghost.

In Mark 3:28–29 we read about *blaspheming* the Holy Spirit: "Verily I say unto you, All sins shall be forgiven unto the sons of men and blasphemies wherewith soever

they shall blaspheme: But he that shall blaspheme against the Holy Ghost hath never forgiveness, but is in danger of eternal damnation." You can blaspheme the name of Jesus and the name of the Father and still be forgiven. But if you blaspheme the Holy Spirit, you have crossed the line. The fifth step is *purposely sinning* after having received the knowledge of the truth. "For if we sin willfully after that we have received the knowledge of the truth, there remaineth no more sacrifice for sins...Of how much sorer punishment, suppose ye, shall he be thought worthy, who hath trodden under foot the Son of God, and hath counted the blood of the covenant, wherewith he was sanctified, an unholy thing, and hath done despite unto the Spirit of grace?" (Heb. 10:26, 29).

Since *quenching* the Spirit is the first step down the road to apostasy, it is important to understand what it means to quench the Spirit. You must first understand the ministry of the Spirit: "Nevertheless I tell you the truth; It is expedient for you that I go away: for if I go not away, the Comforter will not come unto you; but if I depart, I will send him unto you. And when he is come, he will reprove the world of sin, and of righteousness, and of judgment:...He shall glorify me: for he shall receive of mine, and shall shew it unto you" (John 16:7–8, 14). To quench the

Spirit is to resist the things that the Holy Spirit was sent to do.

The Holy Spirit's task is to convict of sin and draw people to Jesus. The Father in heaven abides by His Word and His righteousness and His law. Until you are justified and saved by the Blood of Jesus, you are under condemnation and will perish in hell. But God wants you to be saved; that's why He sent His Son into the world.

Jesus came into the world not to condemn the world, but that the world would be saved. In a way, the Holy Spirit is a mediator between the saving work of Jesus and the justice and judgment of the Father.

Once you become a Christian, the Holy Spirit is always there to speak to your heart, to warn you and to keep you on the right path. The world calls it conscience; but the scriptures state that it is the Holy Spirit who reproves the world of sin, of righteousness and of judgment.

A pastor once told a story about a man who had quit coming to his church. The pastor went to him and asked the reason why. The man replied, "About a month ago on a Tuesday afternoon at about 3 o'clock, I backslid. I was feeding the chickens; and a chicken pecked me on the hand; and I cussed at him. Right there, I backslid, right at that moment." The pastor had to explain that you don't just suddenly, accidentally, without forethought, actually backslide. Rather, true backsliding is a long process of drifting away from God, listening to the world and Satan, and quenching, resisting and grieving the Holy Spirit.

There is more than one way to quench the Spirit. One way is by refusing to exercise the gifts of the Spirit when the Spirit moves upon you. Many churches are Pentecostal in name only, because very seldom are any gifts ever manifested. If the Lord gives you a message in tongues, an interpretation, a word of knowledge, etc. and you refuse to give it, you along with other people have lost a blessing because you have quenched the Spirit.

Another way to quench the Spirit of God is through continual sinning. Even after you're filled with the Holy Spirit, you will still be tempted. It is only sin when you yield to temptation. You are quenching the Spirit when you willfully continue to sin in spite of knowledge of the truth. When temptation comes our way, the voice in our conscience says in one ear, "Don't do that"; meanwhile Satan says, "It's okay. Everybody's doing it." He'll tell you that you can always go back to the altar and pray through next week; that no one will know. We must make a determination to separate ourselves from the world in a life of holiness.

Refusing to read the Bible, to believe the Bible, to obey the Bible is also quenching the Spirit. Many understand the teachings of scripture; yet they live like the devil while claiming to be Christians. The problem in many churches is that people don't really believe the Bible. If you truly believe the Bible is the Word of the Living God, your life will reflect your belief.

It is possible to quench the Spirit with wrong attitudes toward others. For example, there are many in our world who are not as fortunate as you and I. Do you ever walk down the street and see someone begging; and something inside says, "You ought to help"; and something else says, "They can work like I do. I'm not going to give them anything?" The Spirit of God often draws us to help, but we quench His leadings. You are supposed to love everybody—even people who have a different color of skin or who come from a different social class, country or culture. The Holy Spirit can be grieved due to racial and social attitudes.

In the great outpouring of the Holy Spirit at Azusa Street, the church was led by a black pastor; and there were people from many races and backgrounds. The Lord had to deal with racial pride and prejudice. Frank Bartleman said about Azusa Street, "The color line was washed away in the Blood of Jesus." There's something about the Holy Spirit that makes you love people.

Satan subtly hinders spiritual life and ministry through the intellectual quenching of the Spirit. Being filled with the Holy Spirit does not make you immune to intellectualism. Sooner or later the moment will come when someone will say, "Are you one of those tongue talkers? How could you, as smart as you are, and as well-qualified as you are, possibly identify with that crowd?" You may be tempted to turn away from the truth.

God wants you to be a mighty person of God. The Lord wants you to overcome. Some of you have been quenching and grieving the Holy Spirit. If you can overcome the world, the flesh and the devil, your life can be an instrument of God to help reach this generation with the Gospel. Daily abide in Christ through the Holy Spirit; for He "...is able to keep you from falling, and to present you faultless before the presence of his glory with exceeding joy" (Jude 24).

—Excerpts from a message given at CFNI, Dallas, TK.

Harold Vinson Synan is a historian and author, having published a total of sixteen books. He once served as the Director of the Holy Spirit Research Center at Oral Roberts University, as well as General Secretary of the International Pentecostal Holiness Church. Since 1994, he has served as Dean of the School of Divinity at Regent university in Virginia.

Reprinted by permission: Christ for the Nations, CFNI, P.O. Box 769000, Dallas, TX 75376-9000, 800-933-2364.

ASSIGNED ARTICLE

JESUS—THE HEART OF GOD

by Dennis Lindsay

Probably the most disturbing and unsettling truth in the Bible is that Jesus Christ, the son of a simple carpenter from the town of Nazareth, Israel, was in reality God in human flesh. God Himself came near to mankind 2,000 years ago in human form.

"Son of God," when applied to Jesus, means God in the flesh. Christian theology attempts to define the Being of God with three affirmations: (1) There is one God. (2) God exists in three persons. (3) The three persons are the Father, Son and Holy Spirit. All evangelical Christians believe these affirmations and that these three, though distinct persons, are only one God. However, to some it may seem to be a contradiction to speak of one God in three persons.

Some would argue the validity of the Trinity by saying it is ridiculous to maintain that one plus one plus one equals one. Furthermore. it is said to be unscientific and foolish to assume God could be both one personality and three personalities at the same time. Skeptics conclude, therefore, that Jesus wasn't God—that is if God actually exists.

Jesus speaks of Himself and of the Father and of the Holy Spirit. Scripture always presents the order of the Trinity with God the Father first, as the unseen source and the Creator of all things. God, the Son,

second, Who tangibly and visibly reveals the Father to men and executes the will of God. And God the Holy Spirit, third, Who is unseen and yet reveals God the Son to men through the Word of God, through communication with the human spirit and through Spirit-filled believers. This order in scripture is not based on importance nor length of existence, for each member of the Godhead is equally eternal and equally God.

THE PERSONAGE OF THE TRINITY

The primary difficulty in accepting the validity of the Trinity has to do with the meaning of the word "person." What theologians mean by it and what is commonly understood by the word is completely different. In every day usage the word "person" means a separate, distinct individual; but in theological language it is not so. Because this has not been properly clarified, many people believe Jesus is an individual entirely separate from God the Father, which is incorrect. The word "person" 'is actually an imperfect expression of the Godhead inasmuch as the term denotes a separate, rational and moral individual. In the Being of God there are not three individuals—only three personal self-distinctions with the one divine Being. There are three persons in

the Trinity, yet there are no separate forms of distinct individuals.

A GOOD WORKING DEFINITION OF THE TRINITY

The Trinity is not a mysterious, mathematical statement about the Three-in-One, but rather involves the working of God's nature. First. of all, God (the Father) is creative, which was manifested in His creation of man to be the recipients of His love. Second, there are both revelatory and redemptive aspects to God's nature (Jesus). And third, there is an assisting element in His nature (Holy Spirit), which is evidenced by His aiding us to do what we cannot do alone. In other words, God the Father thinks it, God the Son speaks it, and God the Spirit does it.

TRINITY IS IMPERATIVE

The significance of the Trinity is this: If there is no Trinity, God is not love; there could be no love in God because love only exists in the context of relationships. It is absolutely essential to understand the intrinsic value of the Trinity: If the Trinity has not always existed, then God's nature cannot be that of love. If one could go back far enough in time, one would eventually reach the point when there was not yet any created being in existence. If God were alone at this time, without even the other two members of the Trinity then there could have been no love, for love only exists in the contexts of relationships. But since God has always been Three-in-One, He has never really been alone; and love has always been present among the members of the Trinity. Satan, knowing full well the significance of the Trinity, seeks to destroy this indispensable doctrine of truth.

GOD IN CHRIST

Non-Christians who do not have a theological background are often confused by statements such as "the Son of God was sent to be God's provision for sin" or "the second person of the Trinity became the sacrifice for sin." So it cannot be emphasized enough that in Jesus of Nazareth, it was God Himself Who came to redeem us. It was not merely the second member of a triad of individuals who made a personal visit to earth, for "God was in Christ reconciling the world to Himself" (II Cor. 5:19). When we become Christians, we do not enter into three relationships. We enter into a single relationship with one God, Who is known to us as the Father, Who was present in Christ, and Who was made real to us by the Spirit.

The doctrine of the Trinity is not an unscientific, primitive absurdity, but relates intensely to everyday reality. It is interesting that in physics it has been lately observed that the identities of two atomic particles can disappear and their properties merge, yet they remain two individual particles. This is a perfect representation of how God was manifested and revealed by and in His Son, Who as a man was Jesus Christ, and yet is one with the Father.

In the process of salvation, God is not transferring the penalty from one man who is guilty to another who is innocent; God is bearing the penalty Himself. J.B. Phillips states it masterfully in "Good News" (pp. 173–174): "Now if the lonely figure hanging on the cross so long ago were merely a great and good man, martyred for his beliefs, then that is regrettable, but hardly of any significance to us today. But if it was God Who was murdered, if it was God Who willingly allowed the forces of evil to close in upon Him and kill Him, then we are in the presence of something which, though it happened in time, is of eternal significance. We are looking upon something utterly foreign to any other religion. We are seeing God allowing Himself not only to be personally involved in the folly, sin and downright evil of the human situation, but accepting death at the hands of His own creatures."

This is unknown to the majority of people. I believe we must use every skill of communication, every device of writer, artist, poet and dramatist to break the insulation of ignorance and see who died upon the cross. We are without doubt in the presence of an incalculable mystery. It is so far beyond the ordinary man's ideas of God, sin, forgiveness and reconciliation that the mind is carried out of its depth and the heart is overwhelmed by the dreadful significance of the event. Once people begin to realize that the man on the cross is no demigod, no puppet-godling, no fragment piece of Godhead, but God Himself, there is bound to be an explosion in their thinking.

Once we have seen the vision of the crucified God, we begin to see the light which penetrates the darkness of human suffering. The Bible knows no dualism of personality or attitude in God. He who has seen Jesus has seen the God of the Old Testament as well. The Word has always been with God and has also been God. The only change from Old to New Testaments is that the Word became flesh and Jesus revealed the heart of God.

—Excerpts taken from the book *The Trinity of the Godhead.*

Dennis Lindsay is the President and CEO of Christ for the Nations, which was founded in 1970 by his parents, the late Gordon and Freda Lindsay. Dr. Lindsay has written many books on Creation Science, and teaches that subject at Christ for the Nations Institute in Dallas, Texas.

Reprinted by permission: Christ for the Nations, CFNI, P.O. Box 769000, Dallas, TX 75376-9000, 800-933-2364.

LESSON 10

MAIN PRINCIPLE

We can work together in partnership with the Holy Spirit. As we lay aside our fears and our own plans, the Holy Spirit will tell us what to do and say. We are privileged to participate with God as His Spirit moves upon us with words of wisdom, words of knowledge and discerning of spirits.

HOW TO HEAR GOD'S VOICE — IN CHRIST

THE GIFTS OF THE HOLY SPIRIT

The spiritual gifts are manifestations of the Holy Spirit as He moves upon believers to empower them. They are supernatural gifts administered by the Holy Spirit for the common good, using whom He chooses at the time of need.

Revelation Gifts
Word of Wisdom
Word of Knowledge
Discerning of spirits

Power Gifts
Faith
Healings
Miracles

Vocal Gifts
Prophecy
Tongues
Interpretation of Tongues

THE REVELATION GIFTS

The Word of Wisdom

"The gift of the *'word of wisdom'* is supernaturally given by God. It is not *'a'* word of wisdom but *'the'* word of wisdom. It is not just a word on the subject or situation at hand, it is **the word** on it. It is the answer or solution or the will of God in that situation."[1] Remember, these are manifestations of the Spirit (**1 Corinthians 12:7**), not results of man's soul powers.

References that illustrate Jesus' use of the word of wisdom:
Luke 4:3–14; Luke 7:22

The Word of Knowledge

"The *'word of knowledge'* is the supernatural revelation to man of some detail of the knowledge of God. It is the impartation of facts and information which are humanly impossible to know." It is knowledge that is a portion of God's knowledge of facts of the past, present or future. It may reveal the whereabouts of men, warn of coming danger, or expose hypocrisy.[2]

References that illustrate Jesus' use of the word of knowledge:
John 11:11–14; John 4:17–18; Luke 6:8

Discerning of Spirits

The gift of *'discerning of spirits'* is the God-given ability to perceive the presence and activity of a spirit that motivates a human being, whether good or bad. "To 'discern' means to perceive, distinguish or differentiate."[3]

References that illustrate Jesus' use of discernment of spirits:
Matthew 16:22-23; Mark 5:5–13; Matthew 16:15–17

[1] Dick Iverson, The Holy Spirit Today (Portland, Oregon: Bible Temple Publishing, 1987), p.104.
[2] Ibid., pp. 114–115.
[3] Ibid., p. 123.

——Dick Iverson is the Chairman of Ministers Fellowship International, and serves as a spiritual father to many pastors around the world. He is the founding pastor of Bible Temple (now City Bible Church) in Portland, Oregon.

Excerpted by permission from *The Holy Spirit Today* by Dick Iverson. © 1976 by Bible Temple.

LEARNING TO BE SPIRITUALLY DISCERNING

by John Dawson

I first started taking seriously the gift of discerning spirits while listening to the Korean pastor Paul Yonggii Cho. He was speaking at a meeting I attended, describing a personal encounter with an evil spirit. While he spoke, my thoughts turned inward: Jesus seemed to be in constant confrontation with demons, but when was the last time I had exercised the gift of discernment in my circumstances? Not that I didn't in every believer's authority to resist Satan's attacks. At times in my own ministry I had rebuked demonic forces when I sensed that was what circumstances demanded, but was I really embracing all that the Holy Spirit had for me?

Exercising spiritual gifts requires initiative, so as I listened to Yonggi Cho speak, I asked the Lord to give me his view of the unseen realm. "Lord," I prayed, "Do I have blind spots? Are there subtle influences of demonic accusation and deception that I'm missing?"

I continued to ponder these questions during my flight home. Before the conference, two intercessors in two different cities told me that a spirit of accusation was attempting to destroy my family and my ministry. What did that mean? How should I resist it? "I can't become paranoid about demons," I thought. Some people see deliverance as the solution for everything when the problem may really be solved through repentance, or proper management or application of some other wise principle. "Well, Lord," I said, "if there is an actual demon attacking me I trust that you'll show me."

The plane landed. I retrieved my baggage and flagged down my wife as she circled the Los Angeles airport in our family van. As soon as I opened the door, a distinct impression came to me. I felt the oppression of a foul spirit in the van with my wife and three sons-not possessing anybody, just lurking in the background.

As we drove out of the airport, I began to think back over the last six months. There was definitely a pattern of criticism and misunderstanding in some of our non-family relationships. I drove into the parking lot and explained to my family what I was feeling, that some of the conflicts we had faced recently were more than the expected stress of a busy life. As the priest in my home, I joined with my wife in commanding that spirit to go from us, and immediately we sensed the departure of an evil presence.

> DEMONS DON'T LIMIT THEMSELVES TO INDIVIDUALS. OFTEN THEY CARRY ON THEIR WORK BY CONCENTRATING ON SPECIFIC LOCATIONS.

The next day I went into earnest prayer for my staff and the Los Angeles Youth With A Mission headquarters. As I prayed, a picture of the boardroom came into my mind. This is the room in which the directors meet to seek the Lord and make long-range decisions. In my mind's eye I could see a gloomy cloud hovering in a corner next to the ceiling. I realized that I was discerning a spirit of unbelief. "Yes, that's it," I thought. "Every time we meet in there everybody becomes unusually anxious about finances even though God has proved so faithful." I became angry—angry at a spirit that would dare to accuse our generous, faithful, heavenly Father.

During the next few days we carried out a season of spiritual house cleaning. A spirit of confusion that had oppressed a family for months was exposed and sent into the waste places (Mt 12:43) along with several other demons that had been practicing a subtle harassment right in the middle of our Christian ministry.

The gifts of the Spirit are simply the abilities of Jesus just as the fruits of the Spirit represent the personality of Jesus. Jesus lives in you, the believer, and he is able to be in us and through us everything that we are not. He is the source of our victory over sin, our wisdom, strength, love and power. He doesn't give us some love, he is love and he lives his life through us as we yield to his control.

One of the abilities or gifts of Jesus' Holy Spirit within us is the ability to discern or see the activity of spirits in the unseen realm (see 1 Co 12:10). We can choose to exercise this gift, or we can neglect it even though we believe it is biblical.

Sometimes we think that the gifts of the Spirit are the special domain of the super-mature, but the truth is that they are part of God's grace, expressed in order to bring us to maturity. You can and should stir up this gift within you. Discernment may not be your special ministry emphasis, but it should not be neglected in anyone's daily life.

Exercising discernment is much like using the gift of prophecy. Many believers have been used by the Holy Spirit to impart a special word of encouragement to other believers in a home meeting or church service. When this occurs, it is not a result of the Holy Spirit grabbing the person and forcing speech from his or her lips. Instead, the speaker usually senses the beginning of what God wants to say and voluntarily yields to the Holy Spirit in expressing that thought. The person begins in faith out of love for God and his people and as thought follows thought the prophecy moves to completion.

Spiritual discernment is similar in that it requires an act of the will and an act of faith. It takes a childlike humility to act upon the impressions that the Holy Spirit brings us. I feel very vulnerable telling you the story of my family's parking lot encounter with an evil spirit of accusation. That incident departs from the safe ground of the tangible and exposes to you the highly subjective experience of my inner life with God. This kind of unsophisticated vulnerability is essential if we are to see any supernatural manifestation of the Lord's power. Signs and wonders follow steps of obedience to the Master's voice.

NEIGHBORHOOD BATTLES

Demons don't limit themselves to individuals. Often they carry on their work by concentrating on specific locations. Have you ever thought about the battle for your immediate neighborhood? For the last ten years, I have lived in a poor, black neighborhood in Los Angeles. My neighbors and I have a common enemy. Our community is tormented by spirits of despair, hopelessness, depression, discouragement and rejection. Even as I write, my neighborhood is making headlines because of gang

violence and mass arrests. The Bible says that we are not fighting against flesh and blood (Ep 6:12). The devastation of drugs and violence stems from the destruction of the family, and the destruction of the family is accelerated in an atmosphere of despair. What creates atmosphere? Atmosphere is a theatrical term for the collective mood of an audience during a play. In daily life the human spirit is sensitive to a spiritual atmosphere not seen with the eye—whether we realize it or not. Man is, by definition, incarnate spirit and is sensitive to spiritual realities, including the activity of demons seeking to oppress and deceive.

Several years ago my staff and I went on a prayer walk around our neighborhood. We stood in front of every house, and rebuked Satan's work in Jesus' name and prayed for a revelation of Jesus in the life of each family. We are still praying. Our neighborhood has a long way to go, but already we can see tangible social, economic, and spiritual transformation.

There were times when demonic oppression resident in my neighborhood has almost crushed my soul. I received a death threat. My tires were slashed. I was often depressed at the sight of boarded-up houses, unemployed youth, and disintegrating families. But I was determined not to run away.

Today there are six Christian families on the block where I live and there is a definite sense of the Lord's peace. The neighborhood is no longer disintegrating. People are renovating their houses and a sense of community is being established around the Christian families.

But the battle is still with us. Last week a neighbor discovered a loaded pistol in my driveway just before my children came out to go to school. Two doors away, drugs are sold all night from a house belonging to an alcoholic who is unchanged after years of prayer and ministry.

These realities are a challenge to my faith but I believe that as we continue in prayer the demons of hopelessness, violence, and addiction will be driven from this place completely.

NATIONS AND CITIES

All over the world, praying Christians are arriving at a consensus concerning the nature of spiritual battle over their cities. In London, for example, prayer warriors believe that they are warring with a spirit of unrighteous trade that has influenced the world through that great city for hundreds of years .

Whole countries are kept in darkness by Satanic lies that have become cornerstones of a particular culture. Take, for example, the struggle with rejection and the fear of authority experienced by many Australians. Entering through the cruel roots of Australian history, Satan has been able to create general distrust of all authority figures, including the highest authority of all—God himself. The wonderful truth is that Australia is not a nation founded on rejection and injustice, but a chosen people with as much dignity and potential as any people in history—a people greatly loved by a heavenly Father who is calling them to healing and purpose.

In 1979 I witnessed an interdenominational gathering of believers, fifteen thousand strong, make a covenant with God on behalf of their nation. There was an obvious spiritual release when one leader led the crowd in consciously extending forgiveness toward Britain for the injustice and rejection suffered by their forefathers when Britain established Australia as a jail colony. Prophetic revelation about the purpose and destiny of the nation has been pouring into Australia through its national church ever since. Australian Christians have begun to discover many indicators of God at work even in the earliest days of their national history.

What about your city? How will you contribute to victory in its spiritual battle? Here are some ways to determine who your enemy is and how he got his authority:

Study Your City's History. Ask yourself the question, "Why is this city here?" Is it just a product of geography and commerce, or does God have a redemptive purpose in mind? Jonah was surprised at the way God looked at Nineveh. Your city is God's city. Its people are made in his image.   Satan is an invader and the usurper operating in your territory. Look into the history of your city; you may find clues as to what is oppressing the people today. An obvious example of this is the spirit of greed let loose during the California gold rush, which dominates the culture of Los Angeles and San Francisco to this day.

Don't simply examine secular history. Look into the history of God's people in your city, too—particularly during times of revival. God is a covenant-keeping God, and you may be amazed at the promises received by past generations as your spiritual forefathers engaged in similar battles. It is an important principle of humility to acknowledge and honor those who have gone before us. It also inspires our faith. It was because of God's covenant with David that Josiah's generation lived in a time of revival rather than judgment. If you live in Los Angeles, for example, a study of the Azusa Street revival should give you insight into today's battle. During times of revival, the supernatural realm is seen with great clarity, and often records are kept and books written which contain important insights. The battle is not new, and we ourselves are the fruit of the prayerful labor of past generations.

Identify Prophets, Intercessors and Spiritual Fathers. In every city there is what I call a hidden el-

dership. These are the saints that you will not find listed in any human book. They are God's circle of mature believers who pray until victory comes. "I have posted watchmen upon your walls, O Jerusalem," wrote Isaiah, "they will never be silent day or night. You who call on the Lord, give yourselves no rest, and give him no rest till he establishes Jerusalem and makes her the praise of the earth" (Is 62:7-8). Some of these "watchmen" are easy to identify, such as veteran pastors, while others may be intercessors in obscurity. When there is a common theme among these prayer warriors, it reveals God's battle plan. God always confirms a strategy through several witnesses and this is particularly important when dealing with demonic forces.

Get the Facts. I'm often amazed at our ignorance of the basic realities around us. Do you know your city? You should carry a census in one hand and the Bible in the other. What percentage of people actually attend church? How many people are in poverty? Why are they in poverty? Where do they live? Are there subcultures, ethnic groups, changes in the economy, an aging population? Spiritual warfare does not operate independently of other realities.

The prophet Jeremiah exhorted the Jewish exiles in Babylon to "...seek the peace and prosperity of the city to which I have carried you into exile. Pray to the Lord for it, because if it prospers, you too will prosper" (Jer 29:7). This is an exhortation to Jews in Babylon who, like some modern believers, had a tendency to dream of a distant Jerusalem instead of knowing the task at hand. Be grateful for the city in which you live. Study its potentials and thank God for them. Only a grateful heart receives revelation.

STRATEGIES FOR BATTLE

Everything born of God goes through a process similar to the natural process of reproduction: conception, gestation, travail and birth. God's people are prepared to conceive through worship. As we offer thanksgiving and praise to God, he conceives within us his plans for our city.

WE MUST NOT NEGLECT THE OFFENSIVE WEAPONS OF OUR LORD, WEAPONS GIVEN US FOR THE COMMON GOOD.

Wait for Insight. Don't rely on finite reasoning or human cunning. Spiritual battles are won by obeying directions given by the Holy Spirit. If we listen to God with childlike dependency, he will guide us into victory. The Scripture is full of exhortations about waiting on God. In Psalm 40 David recounts: "I waited patiently for the Lord; he turned to me and heard my cry." Or as Jesus promised, he wouldn't leave his sheep without a shepherd who clearly guides them: "My sheep listen to my voice; I know them, and they follow me" (Jn 10:27).

Identify with Sin. We need to identify with the sins of the city in personal and corporate repentance. When Nehemiah prayed for the restoration of Jerusalem, he didn't pray for the city as though he were not part of it. He said, "I confess the sins we Israelites, including myself and my father's house, have committed against you" (Ne 1:6). Another rebuilder, Ezra, went even further: "O my God, I am too ashamed and disgraced to lift up my face to you, my God, because our sins are higher than our heads and our guilt has reached to the heavens" (Ez 9:6). Both of these men lived righteous lives. You may be a righteous person who is not personally involved with the vices present in your city, but there is no temptation which is not common to man (1 Co 10:13). We can all identify with the roots of any given sin.

Take, for example, the shedding of innocent blood in the act of abortion. You may never have participated in an abortion, but all of us have been guilty of the root sins which give place to such an activity. I can think of five common roots that lead to abortion: lust, the love of comfort, the love of money, rejection, and unbelief. These are struggles common to us all, and illustrate, therefore, the basis of honest identification with the sins of our city when we "stand in the gap" asking for God's mercy.

Overcome Evil with Good. Is the enemy tempting us to be fearful and stingy? Let's come against greed with hilarious generosity, or overcome pride with humility, lust with purity, fear with faith.

Travail in Prayer until God's purposes are born. This may be an exercise which is deeply personal and private, or may be a corporate exercise as part of scheduled city-wide prayer meetings. That which is conceived of God will eventually come to birth. Just as the contractions of the uterus herald the beginning of labor, there are times when our souls are stirred by God's spirit to seasons of intense prayer. Anybody who earnestly seeks God experiences such travail, but when the united Christians of a city are at this stage, it is an indicator of impending revival.

In 1984, I was the coordinator of a huge outreach during the Summer Olympics held in Los Angeles. In the year before the outreach, I would often find myself groaning and weeping with the compassion of Jesus for the people of my city. I drove the freeways with tears streaming down my face. Later that year, hundreds of pastors from over 50 denominations joined me in times of intense prayer during outreach planning sessions. During these meetings, we learned and applied the principles I've listed here. The first day of the outreach was like the celebration of a victory already gained. Sixteen thousand people gathered in a praise celebration the night before we hit the streets. The days that followed saw an unparalleled harvest.

Good teaching abounds on the subject of the individual believer's deliverance from evil spirits, but we can't let that become our sole focus in resisting our common enemy. Such a perspective will only contribute to a self-centered spirituality and a mentality that suggests that we're victims rather than overcoming warriors.

Our lives are spiritual battlefields and fiery darts will attack each of us. We must not neglect the offensive weapons of our Lord, weapons given us for the common good. With one hand we resist with our shield of faith, with the other we take new territory as we wield the sword of the Spirit, the Word of God. If we join in unity with other believers, we'll discover the power of an awesome army. Through our steps of faith and obedience we can contribute to a victory much bigger than our own—a victory that includes neighborhoods and cities, a victory that lasts forever.

—John Dawson is part of the leadership team of Youth With a Mission, an international missionary organization of Christians from many denominations dedicated to presenting Jesus Christ to this generation.

ASSIGNED ARTICLE

CULTIVATING THE SPIRIT'S GIFTS

by Jack Deere

IF WE EAGERLY PURSUE GROWTH IN THE LORD AND HIS GIFTS, WE WILL EXPERIENCE
SUPERNATURAL MINISTRY BEYOND ALL THAT WE ASK OR THINK

In the fall of 1987, I helped lead a weekly Bible study at a church in Fort Worth, Texas. At the conclusion of one Wednesday night meeting, we invited people in the group to share publicly anything they thought the Lord had revealed to them that might be edifying for those present.

A young woman in the front row stood up immediately. "The Lord has shown me that a young man is attending this meeting for the first time tonight" Karen said gently. "He is in bondage to pornography. The Lord wants to help him and not embarrass him. He should see one of the leaders afterward so that they can pray for him."

When the meeting was over, an ashen-faced young man came up to me trembling and sweating. "I am the one the young lady was talking about," he said.

This young man had been in bondage to pornography since his early teens. Although he was now a seminary student with a wife and children, he was still in bondage to pornography—in fact, it was stronger than ever. But before the evening was

over, he was making a full confession to me and another pastor, and we were praying for him.

In 1 Corinthians 14, the apostle Paul describes what happened in our Bible study that evening: "If an unbeliever or someone who does not understand comes in while everybody is prophesying, he will be convinced by all that he is a sinner and will be judged by all, and the secrets of his heart will be laid bare. So he will fall down and worship God, exclaiming, 'God is really among you' " (vv. 24–25, NIV).

That seminary student, who had never attended our weekly Bible study before, certainly qualified as "someone who does not understand." He didn't even believe the miraculous gifts of the Holy Spirit were given today. In fact. he had come that night to evaluate our meeting. But God had decided to evaluate him!

Stories such as this are common in churches that welcome and cultivate the Spirit's supernatural gifts. The Lord commands us to "eagerly desire" or "strive after" these gifts, especially the gift of prophecy (1 Cor. 12:31; 14:1, 39).

Each of the miraculous gifts, as well as the other spiritual gifts that are not normally classified as miraculous, are given to us as tools to edify the body of Christ (1 Cor. 12:7). All the gifts have valuable contributions to make to the body. But these contributions will never be made and the growth that could have come to Christ's body will be lost, unless we learn how to cultivate these gifts within the church.

CULTIVATING THE SPIRIT'S GIFTS

Some people have a difficult time understanding how you can cultivate or develop a gift that is supernaturally empowered. This difficulty stems from viewing the miraculous gifts as magical or mechanical. We have no difficulty comprehending that a teacher can grow in the gift of teaching, or an evangelist in the gift of evangelism. So why is it difficult to believe that someone can grow in the gift of healing or prophecy?

The truth is that we can grow in every spiritual exercise and every spiritual gift. As soon as I was

September 1993, Charisma

convinced that the Scriptures taught God gives supernatural endowments today, I began pursuing growth in the gifts of the Holy Spirit. From my Bible study and my own experience, I've identified nine things you can do to cultivate spiritual gifts in your life:

1
DECIDE THAT THE GIFTS ARE VALID AND VITAL

You must be convinced that the Bible teaches the gifts are for today and that they are important; otherwise you won't have faith to exercise them or to pray for them. Likewise, you must be confident that the gifts are given to all Christians (1 Pet. 4:10), not just a few specially deserving people. Once I came to these two conclusions, I was ready to begin cultivating the gifts in my own life.

2
PRAY FOR PARTICULAR GIFTS

Although the Holy Spirit distributes the gifts to each one just as He wills (1 Cor. 12:11), Paul still encouraged the Corinthians to pray for gifts. If you have the gift of tongues, for example, Paul says that you should pray for the gift of interpretation (1 Cor. 14:13).

Don't be passive in regard to your spiritual gifts. Don't say, "The Lord can give me any gift He wants, so I will just wait for Him." That statement may be theologically correct but it often becomes an excuse for passivity.

God could make you a great Bible scholar if He wanted to, but I don't know any great Bible scholars who got that way without diligently pursuing the knowledge of the Bible. Nor do I know any great evangelists who got that way without diligently pursuing evangelism.

Remember: "You do not have, because you do not ask God" (James 4:2). I pray every single day specifically for the spiritual gifts that I want to be operative in my life. For example, healing is one of the gifts that I want to experience regularly in my ministry. So every day I ask the Lord to give me authority and power in this gift. I even specify the kinds of diseases and conditions that I want to see Him heal when I pray for people.

Turn your desires into prayers, and soon you will know the gifts the Lord wants to give you.

3
IDENTIFY YOUR GIFTS

We can identify our spiritual gifts in at least four ways: through our success or lack of success as we attempt to minister with various gifts, through our desires, through the counsel of others and through prophetic impartation of spiritual gifts.

• The areas in which you are most successful are likely to be those areas in which you are gifted. If you repeatedly fail in your attempts at healing but have success in prophesying, that may indicate that you have a prophetic gift rather than a healing gift. Normally, you will have to minister in various areas before you can determine which gifts you have.

• Our desires frequently indicate the gifts that we have or the gifts the Lord wants to give us. When I began desiring to be used in a healing ministry, I had no evidence in my previous ministry that the Lord had gifted me in that way. But as I began praying for the Spirit to use me to heal and then praying for the sick to be healed. I discovered that healing was a gift the Lord wanted to give to me.

• Because it's possible to deceive ourselves, the counsel of others can be an important gauge for de-termining our gifts. I have a friend who has an amazing gift of evangelism, but he is ignoring that gift and trying to become a teacher. In situations like these the counsel of others, especially trusted friends, can save us a lot of frustration and wasted effort.

• Finally, gifts can be given through the laying on of hands with prophetic utterance. Timothy received a spiritual gift "through a prophetic message when the body of elders laid their hands on [him]" (1 Tim. 4:14).

I've witnessed this type of impartation numerous times over the past few years. After John Wimber prayed for me several years ago, I noticed an immediate increase in revelatory words and healings whenever I prayed for people. I've also seen this happen when Paul Cain has prayed for people to receive various spiritual gifts. But this activity must be done under the leadership of the Holy Spirit or nothing will happen.

4
LOOK FOR OPPORTUNITIES TO EXERCISE THE GIFTS

Cultivating spiritual gifts requires attempting to use them on a regular basis. When you begin practicing the gifts of the Spirit, it's helpful to have a non-threatening atmosphere, such as in a home group of 10 to 20 people.

The small size of a home group makes it possible to get to know one another so you feel a degree of security. It's much easier to give a prophetic word in front of 20 people who know and love you than in front of 500 people on Sunday morning who may not know you at all. In such an informal setting, it's also easier to discuss and analyze the ministry attempted that evening.

September 1993, Charisma

More often than not, exercising a spiritual gift involves some risk—specifically the risk of looking foolish. Almost as soon as I began asking God to give me a healing ministry, I began praying for sick people. Most of the sick people I prayed for at first did not get healed. I also had some embarrassing moments when I first began giving revelatory *words* in public. But there is no other way to grow in anything apart from constant practice and risking.

Think of the spiritual gifts in terms of the parable of the talents (Matt. 25:14–30). If we don't risk, our gift will not grow. And if our gift doesn't grow, the Lord will not be pleased with us.

5
STUDY THE GIFTS AND SEEK TRAINING

The Scriptures offer us many helpful principles concerning the miraculous gifts, as well as numerous examples of supernatural ministry that we can learn from. I also read numerous books dealing with the gifts of the Spirit, as well as biographies of Christians who were used powerfully in supernatural ministries. I've found conferences that focus on spiritual gifts to be especially beneficial. The ideal conference of this nature is one whose purpose is to train the participants in the gifts of the Spirit. In these kinds of conferences, you have the opportunity to exercise the gifts of the Spirit, as well as to observe gifted individuals manifesting healing gifts, revelatory words or other supernatural endowments.

Another helpful thing is having friendships with people who are more advanced in the gifts than I am. The Scriptures say: "As iron sharpens iron, so one man sharpens another" (Prov. 27:17). I will forever be indebted to friends like John Wimber and Paul Cain, who have: "sharpened"

me in the area of Spiritual gifts. We tend to emulate our friends (Prov. 13:20), so it's important to cultivate friendships with people you admire and want to be like.

6
DON'T RELY ON FORMULAS OR TRADITIONS

Divine power does not travel in words but in a *personal relationship*. Jesus said, "Apart from me you can do nothing" (John 15:5). We cannot simply expect results because we perform the "right" actions and we say the "right" words.

The seven sons of Sceva, a Jewish chief priest, thought they had discovered the right formula for casting out demons: "In the name of Jesus, whom Paul preaches, I command you to come out" (Acts 19:13–14).

They got the right name, "Jesus." And they had the right Jesus, the one "whom Paul preaches." They even had the right command, "Come out." According to the formula, they had everything right. But the demon did not come out.

Instead the evil spirit overpowered all seven men and sent them running for their lives naked and bleeding! They had the right formula, but they did not have the right relationship.

Jesus gave us the secret to effective ministry when He said. "The Son can do nothing by himself; he can only do what he sees his Father doing, because whatever the Father does the Son does also" (John 5:19). Jesus had to be led by His Father, and so do we.

I have to remind myself of this principle all the time. Sometimes the Lord will lead me to pray a certain way or do a certain thing, and it proves to be effective for someone's healing or for casting out a demon. My tendency is to turn that successful

prayer into a formula. I think that if it worked before, it will work again.

Relying on formulas feels so much more secure than trying to listen to our heavenly Father for moment-by-moment instructions. Yet the One who had the most supernatural ministry of all said, "The Son… can do only what He sees His Father doing" (John 5:19). Jesus must be our model, not our formulas or our traditions.

7
PURSUE SPIRITUAL GIFTS FOR THE RIGHT REASONS

Years ago, while jogging along a river bank, I was asking the Lord to release greater healing gifts in my ministry. Just then, a voice erupted inside my mind: "What do you want these gifts for?"

I recognized that voice immediately as the voice of the Lord, and it offended me. Why would He ask me a question like that? I was pursuing the gifts of the Spirit for Him—and my pursuit of those gifts had cost me dearly.

I slowly realized, however, that an omniscient God does not ask questions for information—the question was intended to expose the condition of my heart. As I pondered His question, my impure motives slowly and painfully emerged. I realized that there was still a great deal of carnality in my desire for supernatural gifts.

One of the greatest mercies that God can give to His children is to show them their sin. Without the revelatory ministry of the Holy Spirit, we cannot understand the motives of our heart (Jer. 17:9–10). But when the divine light exposes our darkness, we can repent, confess and receive His forgiveness (I John 1:9). This is crucial in cultivating spiritual gifts, because our motives are a significant

September 1993, Charisma

factor in the release of power in our lives.

What motivated Jesus to heal and to do miracles? He did miracles to demonstrate that He was God's Son, to show the truth of the gospel, to bring glory to God, to display compassion for the hurting, to open doors for evangelism and so on.

When we share His motives, He can trust us with His power. As I pray for the release of spiritual gifts in my life, therefore, I also pray for the heart and the affections of the Lord Jesus to be released in my life.

8
PUT YOUR CONFIDENCE IN CHRIST

To experience the supernatural ministry of the Holy Spirit, the most important thing you can do is to put your confidence in Christ's power, wisdom and goodness—not your own. After all, the power for miracles is not obtained by our godliness; it was bought with the blood of God's Son.

After recording that Jesus healed all the sick people in Capernaum, the apostle Matthew noted: "This was to fulfill what was spoken through the prophet Isaiah: He took up our infirmities and carried our diseases" (Matt. 8:17). Quoting from Isaiah 53, the great Old Testament chapter that describes the Messiah's substitutionary death, Matthew is teaching us that the power to make whole can only be found in one place: in the cross of Christ.

Don't ever try to talk God into healing someone because that sick person deserves it. No one is made whole because they deserve it. We are only healed because of the goodness of God's Son expressed in His sacrifice for us.

Never make the mistake of thinking that when you pray for someone, it's your personal power or holiness that will bring supernatural help for that person. Remember what Peter told the astonished crowd after the Spirit used him to heal the lame man at the temple gate: "Men of Israel, why does this surprise you? Why do you stare at us as if by our own power or godliness we had made this man walk? ... The God of our fathers has glorified his servant Jesus" (Acts 3:12-13). So put your confidence in Christ rather than in your own goodness or the goodness of those for whom you pray.

You must also put your confidence in Christ's ability to guard you from deception. Unfortunately, much of the church is afraid to try anything different from their traditions because they have more confidence in Satan's ability to deceive than in Christ's ability to lead.

Various occult and New Age movements constitute a serious threat to the church, but dead religious traditions pose a far greater threat to the church. Blind traditionalism draws the very life out of the church and persecutes any new work the Holy Spirit wants to establish among us. It's absolutely imperative, therefore, that we put our confidence in the Lord's ability to lead us, not in Satan's ability to deceive us.

9
BE PATIENT

Don't despise the day of small beginnings. Be thankful for everything you are learning and for every answer to prayer the Lord gives you. Be thankful even for the frustration you feel when things seem to be going too slowly. If you will persist in your pursuit of the Lord and His gifts, more will be given to you than you ever dreamed to ask.

People who want more of God and more of the Spirit's gifts almost always feel that things are moving too slowly. They almost always fear that they will miss out. But if you truly desire more of God and more of His gifts, it is a sign that the mercy of God is resting upon you.

The desire to be used in supernatural ministry was put in your heart by your heavenly Father, and He has not drawn you this far to abandon you or leave you unfulfilled. The holy frustration you feel right now is meant to drive you on. God wants you to be thankful for what you have, but He never wants you to be content with your present level of divine intimacy or power. God wants you, like the apostle Paul, to press on "to know Christ and the power of his resurrection and the fellowship of sharing in his sufferings, becoming like him in his death" (Phil. 3:10).

Why should you be content with anything less?

—Jack Deere has over twenty years of pastoral experience and is currently associate senior pastor on the executive staff at Trinity Fellowship Church in Amarillo, Texas. He is also Dean of the Wagner Leadership Institute in Colorado Springs, Colorado.

Reprinted by permission: Charisma Magazine and Strang Communications Company.

DISCERNING OF SPIRITS

by Judith MacNutt

BY REVEALING TO US THE PRESENCE OF EVIL SPIRITS AND HOLY ANGELS, THIS
UNIQUE GIFT HELPS US MINISTER TO THE TORMENTED
PEOPLE WHO NEED GOD'S HELP.

One afternoon, as my husband, Francis, and I were getting ready to hold a healing service, we heard a weird barking sound coming from the back of the church. Then we saw its source: a young girl being dragged in by a group of people. Earlier, the pastor had told us that the girl's prayer group would bring her to us because they were convinced she was under demonic control. They wanted us to check her out and, possibly, pray for deliverance.

With only 10 minutes until the service was to begin, we took her outside to the courtyard. From what we were observing—her lolling head, her strange yelping sounds—it would have seemed that she did indeed need deliverance. But after closing my eyes and praying a short while, I said: "This is not demonic. She simply has a physical problem—maybe a lesion in her brain. She needs healing, not deliverance."

How did I know? Through the gift of "discerning of spirits" (1 Cor. 12:10). This is an excellent example of how this unique gift of God's grace helps us minister to the tormented people who seek our help.

In our experience, we have found two basic ways to discern the presence of evil spirits:

1. **Natural observation**. As our experience increases in praying for deliverance, we quickly get to know the ordinary ways that evil spirits reveal their presence. Sometimes we can see it when we start to pray:

- A man's eyes roll back in his head until all that can be seen are the whites of his eyes.
- Another man suddenly lurches forward and begins to cough—not an ordinary cough, but a convulsive cough. Then he foams at the mouth and seems to cough up something.
- A woman's hands go rigid and her spine arches back until she is bent in the shape of a bow.

Then there are the sounds we hear:

- A man drops to the ground and starts to roar like a lion.
- Someone may blurt out. "We hate you." (not "I hate You.") or "You'll never get us out!"
- A voice may cry, "This woman belongs to me!"

All these are the strongest possible indications that a person needs deliverance.

2. **Supernatural discernment.** Most of what we observe is far less dramatic and convincing. Often we are uncertain whether we are dealing with demonic oppression or a physical problem—as with the girl who yelped.

Take for example a young man diagnosed with schizophrenia. He spends most days in his room afraid to come out, suffering from terrible hallucinations. Do demons cause the terrifying visions, or does he simply need healing of the childhood trauma that left him with an awful legacy of fear? Is it a physical problem—a chemical imbalance in the brain that can be treated with drugs: Or is the real answer a combination of one or more of these?

November 1992, Charisma

Most people who need deliverance have symptoms that are similarly ambiguous. How do we make an accurate spiritual diagnosis?

Fortunately, God—out of His great love for us and those who suffer—does not leave us in the dark. He knows that casting out demons by guessing at their presence can hurt the people we're trying to help. For example, if we try to cast out a "spirit of depression" that is not there, we may drive a depressed person closer to despair. God also knows that some evil spirits lie low, below the surface, trusting we will overlook them in a person who truly needs deliverance. This is when the spiritual gift of discernment is especially needed.

LEVELS OF DISCERNMENT

Spiritual discernment operates on two levels. For those at the first level, the extent of their gift is simply to know, beyond the shadow of doubt, that an evil spirit is present. How?

Typically, they simply have an intuition, a sense deep in their own spirits, that evil is present. Others don't experience an intellectual knowing or gut feeling; they have a physical sensation.

Noted Anglican preacher Michael Green, for example, has learned that when he feels the hair on the back of his head stand up, God is warning him of the presence of evil. Roben Lindsey, retired pastor of the Narkiss Street Baptist Church in Jerusalem, has come to recognize the same thing when one of his ears begins to burn.

For others, the gift of "discerning of spirits" goes beyond the level of simply detecting that an evil spirit is present to being able to identify what kind of spirit it is. This second level of discernment provides a great advantage.

Knowing the spirit's identity not only allows us to cast it out by name, but, more importantly, it gives us a clue as to how it gained entry into the victim's life. This helps us to minister to the person in that area of weakness.

If, for instance, we identify a "spirit of depression," we can find out how the depression got started and pray for healing. If the spirit is discerned to be "witchcraft" or something on that higher order, we know we will have to probe deeper to find the point of entry for the occult influence in the victim's life. Then, after we lead the person to repent and renounce the spirit, we can command the demons to leave.

The variety of ways that Christians who have a ministry of discernment are able to identify evil spirits is a fascinating testimony to God's creativity:

1. **Sight.** Perhaps the most common way that ministers are gifted is in an ability to "see" spirits—good (angels) as well as bad. Usually this is not an external vision with our physical eyes, though that sometimes happens. More often, it's a kind of seeing "in the spirit."

With experience, we come to recognize who the spirits are. Just as we recognize old friends, we recognize old enemies. The demons may also recognize us from previous exorcism encounters. Once when we were praying for a demonized woman, an evil spirit spoke to me through the woman: "The last time I met up with you was in Jerusalem!"

2. **Hearing.** Still other people "hear" God speak a word to them—for example, "hate" or "depression"—that identifies the tormenting spirit. Again, the word may be heard externally, with our physical ears, but more often it is an interior voice.

3. **Spiritual Insight.** Another way to recognize an evil spirit is by spiritual insight—a kind of knowing or intuition. We must be careful here, however. The question arises: How can we be sure this intuition is God's discernment and not simply our own thought? Subjective ministry may harm people we want to help. Any time we are not sure what spirits (if any) we are up against, we need to be very gentle and minister cautiously.

I believe the way the gift of discerning of spirits developed in my life illustrates how a gift grows in its refinement. My gifting is mainly a discernment by seeing. As a child growing up in my 100-year-old home in Kentucky, I saw—with my eyes—a dark and frightening presence on several occasions. Other people in my home, such as my father, heard things—mysterious footsteps tromping around in an empty room upstairs, for example. (Years later, after learning more about spiritual things, a friend and I blessed the house, and nobody has heard or seen anything since.)

As an adult, after training as a counselor, I would often recognize a supernatural evil presence in some of my clients. Later, I learned how to pray for deliverance—and it was then that my gift of "discerning of spirits" began to fully develop. Rather than just detecting the presence of evil, I could identify different kinds of spirits.

I no longer saw dark presences externally; rather, I began "seeing" spirits when I closed my eyes to pray for the Holy Spirit's guidance. And not only evil spirits—frequently, I would also see comforting angels.

Today, if there is an evil spirit in a person I am counseling, the face of the person fades away as I close my eyes to pray. In its place is a superimposed demonic face.

By experience, I have come to recognize most of the faces. Some of them resemble their names: "Grief" looks sad and tormented; "Witchcraft" has slanty eyes, a contorted mouth and a face like a mask. When several spirits are present, the one I see is the dominant, ruling spirit. If the face is one I haven't seen before, I typically discover its identity by asking the Lord. Sometime the identity is revealed later when I interview the person.

If the spirit is not within, but is oppressing the person from the outside, I see the spirit's form—usually not the face—standing over or behind the person. When praying for deliverance, I may see the spirit move away from the person but not disappear. That means I must pray longer until it finally departs for good.

BECAUSE SPIRITS ARE INVISIBLE, ONLY GOD CAN HELP US "SEE" WHAT WE ARE DEALING WITH.

My experience is only one example of the varied ways in which God gifts His servants to free the oppressed. The Holy Spirit may choose to help you in your ministry in a different way, "but the same God works all of them in all men" (1 Cor. 12:6, NIV). You will have to be sensitive to discover how the Holy Spirit will choose to reveal the presence of evil spirits to you.

This supernatural ability to discern spirits is clearly a tremendous aid in ministering deliverance and healing to people at their point of need. We desperately need the Spirit's help in this area. Because spirits are, by their very nature, invisible, only God can help us "see" what we are dealing with. Even when the external actions of a demoniac make it clear that we are faced with Satan's power, we still need the Holy Spirit's help to identify the spirits and know how and in what order we must deal with them.

SEEING ANGELS

Of course, we must not concentrate so much on evil spirits that we neglect to discern the holy angels who are our allies in this fight against evil. In His struggle at Gethsemane, even Jesus welcomed an angel sent by His Father to comfort and strengthen Him. We, too, must learn to ask the Father to send His protective angels to guard us in our battles.

One morning, when I was working as a counselor, a man walked into my office on his first appointment.

Instantly I sensed evil.

When I routinely asked him what his problem was, he shot back, "I don't have a problem; you do!" He then announced that he was a warlock (a male witch) and that he had been assigned to "stop" me.

He said his "master" was disturbed by what I was doing, by my helping clients through prayer. He boasted about his powers and about how he had used them to kill many people.

Frightened, I began praying in the Spirit. Instantly, I felt the presence of an angel behind me, and a surge of courage swept over me.

"I'm not afraid of you," I blurted.

"You should be!"

"Jesus has defeated the one you serve!" I declared, my fear now totally gone.

Suddenly, unexpectedly, he seemed to be gazing, not at me, but at something beyond and above me. His face changed from arrogance to fear. He jumped up, started screaming and ran out of the room.

I believe the warlock fled because he saw the angel that God had sent to protect me. As the Word says, "No disaster will come near your tent. For He will command his angels concerning you to guard you in all your ways" (Ps. 91:10–11).

Like the other gifts distributed by the Holy Spirit, the ability to discern spirits is a clear manifestation of God's grace and love toward us. Those to whom He has given this gift have a unique ability—and responsibility to develop and use it to minister that love to a dying and tormented world.

—Judith MacNutt and her husband, Francis, are co-directors of Christian Healing Ministries in Jacksonville, Florida. She wrote *Praying for Your Unborn Child* (Doubleday). They frequently hold conferences on healing.

November 1992, Charisma

LESSON 11

MAIN PRINCIPLE

We are privileged to participate with God as His Spirit moves upon us with the gift of faith, gifts of healing and the working of miracles.

THE POWER GIFTS

The Gift of Faith

"The '*gift of faith*' is the God-given ability to believe Him for the impossible in a particular situation. It is not so much the general faith which believes God for provision, etc., but goes a step beyond, where one 'just knows' that a particular thing is the will of God and is going to happen."[1]

"This gift is specifically mentioned in 1 Cor. 12:9, is referred to in 1 Cor. 13:2, and may be included in the thought of 1 Cor. 13:13. Besides these references, the gift of faith is illustrated and seen in its out-working and operation throughout the book of Acts."[2]

References that illustrate Jesus' use of the gift of faith:
John 9:1–7; John 11:11

Gifts of Healing

It is the only gift which uses the plural—"*gifts*." "This indicates that the gift of healing may operate on more than one level. It could refer to the fact that different kinds of sicknesses require different kinds of healings and various levels of faith. Some healings, for example, may involve underlying attitudes that must be dealt with before the body will respond. Other healings need an outright miracle. Some healings are instantaneous and others are gradual."[3]

References that illustrate Jesus' use of the gifts of healing:
Mark 1:31; Mark 8:22–25

The Gift of Miracles

"A '*miracle*' is a happening or event which is supernatural; the performance of something which is against the laws of nature. A miracle could be called a supernatural phenomenon. Miracles defy reason and transcend natural laws."[4] "The 'gift of miracles' is simply the God-given ability to co-operate with God as He performs miracles."[5]

References that illustrate the use of the gift of miracles:
John 5:8; Acts 3:6–8, 12; Colossians 1:11

[1] Dick Iverson, *The Holy Spirit Today* (Portland, Oregon: Bible Temple Publishing, 1987), p. 129.
[2] Ibid.
[3] Ibid., p. 137.
[4] Ibid., p. 147.
[5] Ibid.

—Dick Iverson is the Chairman of Ministers Fellowship International, and serves as a spiritual father to many pastors around the world. He is the founding pastor of Bible Temple (now City Bible Church) in Portland, Oregon.

Excerpted by permission from *The Holy Spirit Today* by Dick Iverson. © 1976 by Bible Temple.

ASSIGNED ARTICLE

THE GIFT OF FAITH

by Mahesh Chavda

THE GIFT OF FAITH BRINGS FORTH A SPRING OF BELIEF FROM WITHIN AND PROPELS US TO OPERATE IN THE SUPERNATURAL REALM.

The noonday sun of Kinshasa, Zaire, blazed down on the 30,000 people gathered in Kasavubu Square. I had just finished teaching about prayer and fasting on this third day of a week-long campaign in June 1985. As I stepped back from the microphone, a stillness enveloped me. Suddenly, I saw nothing, felt nothing, heard nothing.

Then I became aware of that quiet voice I had come to know and love. *There is a man here whose son died this morning,* the internal voice said. *Call him up, for this day I want to do something wonderful for him.*

There was no struggle, no anxiety, no uncertainty. I sensed only an infusion of His presence. In that presence was a confidence that this amazing creative miracle was a certainty! Stepping to the microphone, I spoke what had been revealed to me by the Holy Spirit. "If that man can hear my voice," I said, "he must come to the platform."

Out of the crowd quickly emerged a tall, handsome African man. "It's me!" he shouted, running toward me. "I am the man whose son died this morning!"

Earlier that day, Mulaamba Manikai of Mikondo had come to the crusade grounds from Mama Yemo Hospital, where he had left the dead body of his 6-year-old son, Katshinyi (see July 1991 issue of Charisma). Doctors had pronounced the boy dead of cerebral malaria at 4 a.m.

When he reached the platform where I stood, Mulamba took the stairs two at a time and grasped my extended hand. Then I placed my hands on the top of his head and prayed: "In the name of Jesus, I bind the powers of death and darkness that are at work in this man's son.

Holy Spirit, I ask You to go now and resurrect him."

Mulamba's wife and older brother had been sitting at Mama Yemo Hospital, holding the boy's lifeless body in their arms. The moment I prayed, the dead boy suddenly sneezed twice and woke up, as if from a sleep. Looking around, Katshinyi said, "Where's my Papa?" Then he asked for food to eat.

On another occasion, while ministering at a service in Maryland, God revealed to my spirit that He was healing someone's sister of endometriosis. Operating in the gift of faith, I spoke it out. That sister, Tracy, was miles away in Virginia. God was healing her right then. Tracy had suffered from severe endometriosis and was subsequently unable to conceive. Laying hands on Tracy's sister, I prayed: "Heal Tracy now, Lord Jesus. Take away that pain and give her children."

Exactly nine months and two days later, Tracy and her husband rejoiced as she gave birth to a beautiful baby girl!

This Virginia couple was able to cuddle their first baby, and the young African boy's life was restored to him because of a powerful gift that God has made available: the gift of faith. While the operation of this gift will always remain something of a mystery, we can identify certain characteristics of this gift both from Scripture and experience.

MIRACULOUS FAITH

In both instances that I've recounted, the miraculous gift of faith (1 Cor. 12:9) was in operation the second

November 1992, Charisma

I opened my mouth and affirmed verbally what God had revealed to my spirit. Faith operates at a specific moment in time and releases the power of God to accommodate a supernatural act. It is a gift of power that operates along with other gifts of the Holy Spirit.

The New Testament describes three kinds of faith. While all three are of the same substance (Heb. 11:1), each is different in its workings. One kind of faith is essential for salvation (Eph. 2:8); a second kind of faith is part of Christian character that develops in our lives (Gal. 5:22); and a third kind is a miraculous faith that represents a tiny portion of God's total faith (1 Cor. 12:9).

The third kind of faith, the miraculous gift of faith, works under the anointing of the Holy Spirit. Its position in the list of nine gifts, prior to healings and miracles, indicates that it prepares the way for those works. So the Holy Spirit's impartation of the gift of faith can give one the supernatural ability to appropriate a miracle like Tracy's healing from endometriosis or young Katshinyi's resurrection from the dead.

Hebrews 11 lists a number of Old Testament examples of miracles effected through faith: "Through faith (they) conquered kingdoms, administered justice, and gained what was promised: (they) shut the mouths of lions, quenched the fury of the flames, and escaped the edge of the sword…Women received back their dead, raised to life again" (vv. 33–35, NIV). These examples give an idea of the kinds of miracles the gift of faith is able to accomplish.

Yet mighty faith may not always provide deliverance from difficulties; it may provide the courage and endurance to undergo suffering for Christ's sake: "Others were tortured and refused to be released, so that they might gain a better resurrection. Some faced jeers and floggings, while still others were chained and put in prison" (vv. 35–38). Likewise the gift of faith might provide the power to trust God in the midst of persecution.

The New Testament contains many illustrations of the exercise of supernatural faith. For example, Jesus operated in the gift of faith when He calmed the storm, when He cast out evil spirits and when He called Lazarus from the grave. Peter operated in the gift of faith when he raised Dorcas from the dead (Acts 9:36–42). Paul operated in the gift of faith when he told the crew of a storm-tossed ship that God had promised they would survive (27:13–38).

The gift of faith brings forth a spring of belief from within and propels us to operate in the supernatural realm. It is a present-tense faith, sensing that God will make a special event happen, knowing that nothing is impossible (Matt. 17:20).

How much of this faith does one need for a miracle? Only the equivalent of a mustard seed. Jesus said, He exhorted His disciples to have faith in God and told them that unwavering faith could command insurmountable obstacles to move: "If anyone says to this mountain, 'Go, throw yourself into the sea,' and does not doubt in his heart but believes that what he says will happen, it will be done for him" (Mark 11:23).

The gift of faith hinges on speaking. The scriptural pattern of the operation of faith through speaking begins at creation (Gen. 1:3). God's faith is expressed through the words He speaks (Heb. 11:3), and when He speaks, His words, come to pass (Ezek. 12:25).

WHEN THE GIFT OF FAITH OPERATES, I CONSISTENTLY NOTICE A PREVAILING SENSE OF PERFECT CALM, EVEN IN AN ATMOSPHERE OF TURMOIL, OPPOSITION OR APPARENT DISASTER.

When we operate in the gift of faith, we also must speak. Sometimes we may speak to the Lord on behalf of someone else. At other times, we may speak to a person or to an object on behalf of the Lord. In healing campaigns in the United States and overseas, the Holy Spirit requires me to speak out the miracles He quickens to me as they are taking place in the meetings. When the gift of faith operates, I consistently notice a prevailing sense of perfect calm, even in an atmosphere of turmoil, opposition or apparent disaster.

Casting out demons also works through the gift of faith. On various occasions, I have spoken to people under demonic oppression. The demons frequently cry out as they leave, and often the demoniacs will be overcome by the Spirit and fall into a type of sleep. As the person then comes to, he or she is free from the oppression. Although dramatic and potentially disturbing manifestations of screaming, vomiting and body contortions often accompany the miracle of deliverance from evil spirits, the presence of the gift of faith brings a sense of perfect calm.

Infusion is a term that best describes the dynamic at work in the gift of faith. Besides revealing His immediate will through a vision or inner voice, God also gives an infusion of calm, power and confidence—an internal knowledge that the act of God is coming to pass as the spoken words proclaim it. This dynamic is significantly different than when a person decides he or she wants something to happen and speaks in accordance with that desire. In the case of the genuine gift of faith, God initiates the action, and our words accompany what He is doing.

FAITH BEGINS WITH OBEDIENCE

The background for the gift of faith is Jesus' promise of the Holy Spirit: "Anyone who has faith in me will do what I have been doing. He will do even greater things than these, because I am going to the Father...And I will ask the Father, and he will give you another Counselor" (John 14:12–16).

As believers, the key to operating in the gift of faith is our relationship with the Holy Spirit. Developing a relationship with the Holy Spirit, and therefore being prepared to move in the gift of faith, involves three essentials: (1) obedience to His voice (2) brokenness and (3) humility.

Every person who wants to move in the gift of faith must develop a living relationship with the Holy Spirit by taking baby steps of recognizing and obeying His voice. As we accomplish simple tasks, showing ourselves "faithful with a few things" (Matt. 25:21), He assigns us greater and greater works.

When the gift of faith is manifested, the result in a mature believer is a sense of awe and complete humility. The vessel is overwhelmed with the realization that God has done this work, and only God receives the glory.

The gift of faith, like all gifts of the Holy Spirit, has been given to us to fulfill the Great Commission before the coming of the Lord. In anticipation of His imminent return, the Holy Spirit is preparing the bride of Christ. He is raising up an army of men and women who will move in the anointing to do the works of Jesus. Many will be appointed to do special tasks, and they will receive the gift of faith necessary to perform thee tasks.

Although faith itself cannot be seen with the naked eye, its workings can be. Simply to pronounce a miracle, assuming that its fulfillment will automatically follow, is a mistake of presumption. But when the words are spoken from a Spirit-given faith, the workings of such a gift are limitless: "Nothing," said Jesus, "will be impossible to you."

—Mahesh and Bonnie Chavda lead Chavda Ministries International, a worldwide apostolic ministry. The vision of CMI is to proclaim Christ's kingdom with power, equip believers for ministry and usher in revival, preparing for the return of the Lord. Together, the Chavdas pastor All Nations Church in Charlotte, NC. They also spearhead a global prayer movement, The Watch of the Lord®.

Reprinted by permission: Charisma Magazine and Strang Communications Company.

ASSIGNED ARTICLE

GIFTS OF HEALINGS

by Mark A. Pearson

JESUS' HEALING MINISTRY HAS BEEN ENTRUSTED TO THE ENTIRE BODY OF CHRIST IN VARYING DEGREES, NOT JUST TO A FEW PROMINENT "HEALING" MINISTERS.

Donald Duck's mother wears "combat boots." Hardly words that will live in history, but they were significant to me. They represented dramatic, though humorous, confirmation of a miraculous healing I was privileged to be involved in.

I was praying for the sick in the chapel of an Episcopal missionary hospital in the Philippines. Assisting me was the hospital's chief of surgery, Dr. Ron, a devout Catholic physician who wanted to learn more about integrating healing prayer with medical practice.

Among those who came forward for prayer that day was a Filipino man who had lost his hearing. A degenerative illness had destroyed some specific anatomical parts in his ears. Short of a direct intervention of God, he would never hear again.

I placed my hands on his ears and said a simple prayer. As I prayed, he began to speak. Since my fluency in the Tagalog dialect is limited to "When's lunch?" I couldn't understand his words. But I could tell that his speech was not the distorted speech of the deaf; it had the quality of a hearing person.

When I turned to Dr. Ron to find out what the man was saying, his eyes were as big as saucers. "He says he can hear!" my friend said. "But I know apart from God he can't. He's my patient, and there's no way he can hear unless God did a miracle."

"Do you think he's lip reading or somehow picking up vibrations?" I asked. I had no trouble believing in miracles of healing. God had used me in many miracles previously, but I wanted to be sure. "Let's test it out," I continued. "Dr. Ron, send him to the back of the chapel, ask him to face away from us, and tell him to repeat a sentence after me."

Why on earth I picked Donald Duck and dragged his poor mother into it I don't know, but the man duly repeated what I said. That silly sentence confirmed a physical healing that was unquestionably a miraculous intervention of God.

Was the healing a result of my own power or piety? No. It was simply a case of the Holy Spirit manifesting a gift of healing through a person God had chosen as a channel of His love and power.

GIFTS OF HEALINGS

When we speak about a spiritual "gift," we think about God using a person in some special way, often in a way different from his or her natural talent or ability. I know a person, for example, whom God uses incredibly to give sage, practical wisdom to people undergoing confusion or crisis. One knows immediately this is a working of the Spirit because when she isn't under the anointing of the Spirit, she has little wisdom at all!

So it is with a gift of healing. Someone frequently used by God in the gift of healing sees healings taking place regularly, often quickly, sometimes dramatically. One can neither buy this gift nor study for it. But what wonderful things happen when the Spirit is manifested through an individual for this ministry! Illnesses cease, crooked limbs are straightened, emotional problems go away, fatal diseases disappear.

Many times this gift is communicated through the laying on of hands. Some people experience a transfer of power, like an electric current or a surge of warmth, flowing from the minister of the gift to the sick person. Sometimes the healing occurs through a Spirit-prompted word of authority or a command directed to the oppressing disease. Often, though the gift of healing comes through a simple, specific prayer after a time of counseling.

The apostle Paul's list of spiritual gifts in 1 Corinthians 12 literally speaks of "gifts of healings" (v.9). The double plurals indicate different kinds of illnesses that require diverse types of healing, implying there may be varieties and subcategories of this gift. Just as there are general practitioners and specialists in the medical profession, I have found some people in the ministry of healing who pray effectively for a variety of problems and others whose ministry is more focused on one particular ailment or one particular kind of person.

I've seen this often during the years that I've been involved in this ministry. I know one man, for example, who is used in ministering to people with back problems. When Fred prays for them, they often are healed. Yet he doesn't show nearly the same giftedness in praying for people with heart disease, asthma or other ailments.

The Spirit uses another friend to minister healing to children in a far greater way than in ministering to adults. I know another individual who is particularly gifted in ministering emotional healing but not physical healing.

Why does this happen, besides the obvious right God has to use people as He sees fit? I believe the Spirit distributes gifts of healings among believers to keep us humble and to keep us dependent on one another. By using us in only certain aspects of healing ministry, God discourages spiritual pride and teaches us the interdependency we have within the body of Christ.

THE HEALING BODY OF CHRIST

Believers need to recognize that Jesus' healing ministry has been entrusted to the entire body of Christ, not just to a few prominent ministers with extraordinary healing gifts. This point was brought home to me in a humorous way.

Several years ago, I was one of the speakers for a conference in Billings, Montana. During the Saturday morning coffee break, I overheard one of the conference participants sharing with her friend that she was in some pain because of a lingering shoulder ailment.

I butted into their conversation and said to her:

"I couldn't help overhearing what you just said. I'd be happy to pray with you for healing, if you wish." Noticing her puzzled look, I continued: "You just heard the lecture about the gifts of the Spirit. Jesus is still healing people today."

"I know that," she replied. "Fr. Ralph DiOrio, the Catholic healing priest, is coming to Billings in about six weeks. I'm so looking forward to that service. I believe God will heal me through his ministry! That man is so used of God."

I tried to convince her that, while God indeed uses Ralph DiOrio, He uses many others as well. He might use me or several of us. She might not have to wait six weeks. At the very least, we wouldn't make her any sicker for our efforts! She politely declined my offer.

I don't know whether she was healed when Ralph DiOrio came to Billings, nor do I know if she would have been healed had we prayed during the conference. I do know that she had a narrow view of whom God could use to minister healing.

Some believers are frequently used to minister healing and may be considered to "*have* gifts of healings" (1Cor. 12:30, emphasis mine). But the Spirit may choose to manifest a gift of healing through any believer at any point of need. And besides those with special gifts of healing, God also uses those with other gifts of the Spirit to accomplish His healing work.

When I was asked to recruit, train and supervise a healing ministry team for St. Paul's Episcopal Church in Malden, Massachusetts, in the summer of 1982, I faced a classic chicken-and-egg dilemma: I wanted to put those people gifted in healings on the healing team, but how would I know who was gifted if few of the people in the church had any experience in praying for the sick?

The Lord led me to teach a six-week course on Christian healing to anyone who wanted to attend. From that, I invited some of them to stand with me and minister healing at our Friday evening praise service. Lacking any evidence as to who might have a ministry of healing, I went on the basis of their surrender to God, openness to the Holy Spirit and willingness to come under the authority of the church's leadership.

What took place on those Friday nights was an eye-opener to us all. As I prayed regularly with a four-person team—let's call the other members Ruth, John and Ida—other spiritual gifts besides healing were manifested. God orchestrated the manifestation of these gifts in such a way that healing took place, though I believe on many occasions a gift of healing wasn't specifically manifested. Let me give you an example:

One evening, a man came to our prayer station at the front of the church. Even as he walked toward us,

November 1992, Charisma

Ruth sensed within herself that this man, though appearing to be in fine shape, was hurting deeply. Ruth reached out her hands toward him and radiated the love and mercy of God.

Ruth's loving manner enabled the man, whom I'll call Ed, to relax a bit and trust what we were doing. But he was still unable to state his need. After a few moments of watching him struggle, John looked him right in the eye and said, "You're afraid your company will force you into retirement and you won't be able to provide for your family, aren't you?

Ed responded that this, indeed, was his concern and that he was glad John had said it because he knew he couldn't. The four of us then prayed God would work a miracle of some sort to help him in his circumstances. We also prayed that, whatever else happened, Ed would receive an emotional healing for his feelings of inadequacy and shame, and that he would draw closer to God.

Then Ida, usually a quiet person, piped up: "I believe there are a few things you could be doing right now to help the situation and yourself." After listening to her suggestions, Ed responded: "I've never thought of these things. But after hearing them, I believe you're right."

In that brief time of ministry, several spiritual gifts were used. God showed Ed's deep inner state to Ruth through a prophetic insight. Then came the gift of mercy, as she offered God's tender comfort to someone in pain. John then manifested the gift of a supernatural revelation as to the nature of Ed's concern. Finally, Ida exhibited a word of wisdom as she applied truths to a specific situation. Although no specific gift of healing was clearly displayed, the other spiritual gifts working together brought healing to Ed's life.

However they are manifested, healing gifts are a direct result of our heavenly Father's enduring love for His children. While we may continue to grapple with the difficult question of why everyone isn't always healed of every sickness, we can only respond with heartfelt gratitude each time someone is made whole.

No matter how many times I have been used in healing over the years, I always see it as the expression of Jesus' compassion for the sick and suffering. And each time, I stand in awe of God's choice to use men and women as His vehicle to deliver His mercy through gifts of healings.

—Mark A. Pearson, an honorary canon in the Episcopal Church, is president of the interdenominational Institute for Christian Renewal. He conducts numerous conferences on healing and spiritual growth.

Reprinted by permission: Charisma Magazine and Strang Communications Company.

November 1992, Charisma

WORKING OF MIRACLES

by Reinhard Bonnke

GOD'S POWER IS MIRACLE POWER, AND CHRISTIANITY IS A MIRACLE MOVEMENT FROM START TO FINISH.

I started out 20 years ago as a missionary in the tiny African nation of Lesotho. Although people got saved and baptized, the numbers were few. I yearned for a visitation of God that would shake people out of their lethargy, demonstrate that Jesus is alive, and cause men and women to come to the Lord in great numbers. So I invited to our church a prominent evangelist known for his miraculous ministry.

On the first evening of the crusade, our church was packed. I was confident that those who had trusted in witchcraft would see now what the King of kings could do. How I longed to see the sick healed by the power of God.

But as the evangelist preached, I sensed that something was just not right. Then, halfway through the meeting, he urged me to close the service, "I cannot do that," I said. "These people want you to pray for them." But he continued to press me. "All right," I finally agreed. "But you must promise to pray for them tomorrow morning."

On Sunday morning, hopeful that this day would be better, I hurried to where the evangelist was staying, only to find him climbing into a waiting car.

"What's happening?" I asked anxiously. The evangelist looked me straight in the eye and said, "The Holy Spirit told me I must go."

As he drove off, I cried out to God, "I am not a big-name preacher—I am just a missionary, one of your little men," I said. "But now I will preach at this meeting, and You, dear Lord, will have to do the miracles.

As I began to preach that Sunday, an anointing of the Holy Spirit fell upon the people. My interpreter broke down crying in the middle of the message, so great was the presence of the Lord.

Then I heard the Holy Spirit telling me to pray for blind eyes to be healed. When I did, a woman in the crowd shrieked, "I can see! I can see!"

Miracle followed miracle. By the end of the service, I had learned an important lesson: The *anointing of God is distributed as the Almighty sees fit*. He can use the unknown, as well as the known.

It also proved a truth later found in the Word of God: *When the need is there, the gift is there*. You don't get the gift of miracles and carry it around for years, scouting for somebody to give you a chance to use it.

POWER FOR MIRACLES

When the disciples were baptized in the Holy Spirit on the day of Pentecost, they received power just as Jesus had promised: "You will receive power when the Holy Spirit comes on you; and you will be my witnesses" (Acts 1:8, NIV). The distinct purpose of that outpouring was to empower them for ministry, to equip them for fulfilling the Great Commission.

This is a divine contract: "All authority has been given to Me in heaven and on earth. Go therefore and make disciples of all nations," Jesus said. "And these signs will follow those who believe: In My name they will cast out demons, they will speak with new tongues, they will lay hands on the sick, and they will recover" (Matt. 29:19–19; Mark 16:17–20 NKJV).

The risen Christ didn't tell us He had all authority and power just for our interest and information. Would a

November 1992, Charisma

wealthy man show his bulging wallet to a hungry beggar, only to walk away without giving the poor man a dime? Certainly not! So then, Christ told us of His power because all that He has is available to His children—and if ever a task needed miracle power, it is the task Jesus gave His followers.

God's power is miracle power, and Christianity is a miracle movement from start to finish. As the apostles were obedient to God's calling, "many wonders and signs were done" through them (Acts 2:43). Soon after Pentecost, for example, Peter and John healed a man lame from birth at the temple gate (Acts 3:1–10). Later, the sphere of miraculous ministry extended beyond the 12 apostles to Stephen (Acts 6:8), Philip (8:6), Barnabas (13:50–14:3) and other "workers of miracles" throughout the church (1 Cor. 12:28–29).

Although those who worked miracles had not asked specifically for the gift, miracle power was part of the package deal of the Great Commission and Pentecost. If they did what Jesus commanded, Jesus would do what He promised.

NOT IMPULSE, BUT PROPULSION

The only Bible reference to the gift of miracles is 1 Corinthians 12:10: "to another the working of miracles." Derived from two Greek words meaning "energy" and "potency," the gift could be literally translated "workings of powers."

DIVINE WORKS OF POWER REFLECT GOD'S HANDIWORK: THEY ARE LIFE-CHANGING, NOT MERE MAGIC.

At Pentecost, the disciples received *dynamis*, meaning potency. That type of power is a latent force waiting to be drawn upon. When the need arises and we act in faith, that "dynamis" potential explodes into energy. It is like turning the key in the ignition of your car: the unseen power in your battery becomes electrical energy that surges into your started motor, and your engine turns. That is not an impulse; it is a propulsion.

Translators use the word "miracle" to describe this manifestation of the "workings of powers." That word "miracle" actually comes from a Latin term used to describe fairy-tale magic in the Greek and Roman myths. But the "workings of powers" is different.

Divine works of power reflect the mind and heart of God. They are never pointless spectacles to make people gape. They are life-changing, not mere magic.

The gift of miracle-working power operates mainly in the realm of physical need. The vast majority of New Testament miracles involve bringing wholeness to people's bodies and lives: healing diseases, restoring the blind and the lame, casting out demons and even raising the dead.

Although the Gospels record that Jesus turned water into wine, stilled storms, multiplied food and walked on water, there are no New Testament accounts of the disciples doing those same things. Paul, for example, did many miracles of healing and deliverance, but didn't still the storms that left him shipwrecked three times (2 Cor. 11:25). God may sometimes perform nature miracles today, but it is the miracles of healing, restoration and deliverance that are in abundant supply.

God's miracles are signs of His kingdom. They are fingerprints of His wisdom, His love and His mercy. God never acts out of character. So every miracle is in harmony with the revelation of God in Christ and with Christ's passion, death and resurrection.

NO ANOINTED COUCH POTATOES

God often works His miracles through the most unlikely people—such as Philip the table-waiter. The apostles chose Philip as one of seven men assigned to distribute food to the Greek widows (Acts 6:1–5). He was "of good reputation, full of the Holy Spirit and wisdom"—wonderful qualifications for waiting on tables. But Philip discovered his greater potential as he worked diligently to serve God.

After the church in Jerusalem was scattered, Philip went to Samaria and preached Christ. There the Lord worked miracles through Philip, and "unclean spirits, crying with a loud voice, came out of many who were possessed; and many who were paralyzed and lame were healed" (Acts 8:7).

I believe Philip is a good illustration of the kind of person God uses to do miracles: the Bible makes it clear that Philip was a faithful worker and a zealous witness. As he worked diligently to preach the good news, God empowered him to work miracles.

Unless we obey and go where there's a work to do, the gifts of the Spirit are superfluous. Go first, then the gifts come. They are not for armchair Christians. There is no such thing as an anointed couch-potato.

But here is a key. In order to experience the miracle-working power of God, we must listen to and obey the voice of the Spirit. This principle is clearly seen in one

November 1992, Charisma

of the memorable miracles in the Gospels—Peter walking on the water (Matt. 14:22–33).

Peter was exactly where Jesus put him—in the boat. From that position, he could step out on the sea into the miracle area where Jesus was, but only when commanded by Christ.

Note that he made no attempt to do it until Jesus said, "Come!" Peter's faith and action rested wholly on the word of Christ's command.

Presumption is not faith. Nor is bumptious self-confidence. God is not obligated to back you if you're showing off and on some ego trip.

We must patiently wait for God's moment. When I enter a meeting, I am praying in my heart, *Lord, which way is the anointing of the Spirit flowing. Where is the key miracle for today?* Remember, without Him we can do nothing.

GOD'S FINGERPRINTS

To understand the most important qualification for working miracles, I believe the best example to look at is the ministry of Jesus.

When Jesus came, He was found among the poor, the beggars, the wretched, the riffraff. He lavished love upon the unloved. He healed for no other reason than kindness.

Why, for example, did Christ raise the dead son of the widow of Nain? We read He had compassion on the mother and said, "Don't cry." Then He raised her son to life and "presented him to his mother" (Luke 7:11–17). The purpose was not to prove anything; it was simply pure compassion. God doesn't heal just to make a point. Incarnate love has no ulterior motives.

Jesus knew these powerful works would lead people to salvation—His ultimate act of compassion on us sinners. The authentic ministry of the miraculous begins with compassion for the suffering. We must have the same motivation that Jesus did.

So then, to what kind of people is God's gift of miracles readily available? Those who:
* are faithful in what God's called them to do;
* are zealous for the gospel;
* are serving in situations where miracles are needed to do His work;
* are willing to obey the command of Christ;
* have compassion for the suffering.

In our African crusades, when at times 500,000 people are present, the Spirit performs many mighty works. God has a manifold purpose for pouring out those miracles: It's to minister to people who know nothing of Jesus, let alone of His mighty deeds. It's to destroy the works of the enemy wholesale, terrorizing Satan and his minions. It's to reveal the glory of God and to demonstrate His power and love.

When I see miracles happening—miracles of healing, miracles of deliverance, miracles of changed lives—I know Jesus is present. These wonders are His hallmark. That was the way he ministered when he was on earth, and that is the way He ministers now through the Holy Spirit. So long as Jesus remains unchanging—and until He returns in power and glory—the gift of the working of miracles will remain in the church.

—Reinhard Bonnke is a German charismatic evangelist, principally known for his gospel "crusades" throughout Africa. Bonnke has served as head of Christ for All Nations, a ministry headquartered in Frankfurt, Germany and has been a missionary in Africa since 1967. He has written many books which have been printed in different languages.

November 1992, Charisma

LESSON 12

MAIN PRINCIPLE

When the Holy Spirit moves upon us with His vocal gifts, we can make evident God's specific word for our time and place.

THE VOCAL GIFTS

Prophecy

"The *gift of prophecy* is speaking under the direct supernatural influence of the Holy Spirit. It is becoming God's mouthpiece, to verbalize His words as the Spirit directs. The word '*prophecy*' used in 1 Corinthians 12:10 is the Greek word '*propheteia,*' and means '*speaking forth the mind and counsel of God.*' It is inseparable in its New Testament usage with the concept of direct inspiration of the Spirit."[1]

References that illustrate the use of the gift of prophecy:
Luke 1:67; Acts 2:11

The Gift of Tongues

"The *gift of tongues* is the God-given enablement to communicate in a language one does not know, to be interpreted in the assembly that all may understand."[2]

"Again, this is a '*manifestation of the Spirit*' (1 Corinthians 12:7), and not human ability. It has absolutely nothing to do with natural linguistic ability, eloquence of speech, or a new sanctified way of talking."[3]

References to the use of the gift of tongues:
1 Corinthians 14:27–28; 1 Corinthians 14:39–40

Interpretation of Tongues

"The *gift of interpretation* is the supernatural, spontaneous ability to interpret a communication given in tongues into the language understood by the people present. Again, it has absolutely nothing to do with natural knowledge of languages, but comes directly from the Holy Spirit. (1 Corinthians 12:10)."[4]

It is an *interpretation*, not a translation! The purpose of tongues and interpretation is to be a sign to the unbeliever and to provide "edification, exhortation and comfort to the believer. (1 Corinthians 14:3-5). Tongues with interpretation is equal to prophecy."[5]

References to the use of the gift of interpretation:
1 Corinthians 14:5; 1 Corinthians 14:13

---

[1] Dick Iverson, *The Holy Spirit Today* (Portland, Oregon: Bible Temple Publishing, 1987), p. 155.

[2] Ibid., p. 169.

[3] Ibid.

[4] Ibid., p. 173.

[5] Ibid., p. 171.

—Dick Iverson is the Chairman of Ministers Fellowship International, and serves as a spiritual father to many pastors around the world. He is the founding pastor of Bible Temple (now City Bible Church) in Portland, Oregon.

Excerpted by permission from The Holy Spirit Today by Dick Iverson. ©1976 by Bible Temple.

PROPHECY: GOD SPEAKS THROUGH ORDINARY PEOPLE

by Kim Clement

Twenty-one years ago, the Lord rescued me from a life of drugs, rebellion and self-destruction. Though I was only 17 and already a successful musician, I was empty and miserable. I knew I was headed down a dangerous path.

One evening I decided to numb my mind at one of the rock' n' roll clubs in Port Elizabeth, South Africa. As soon as I arrived, I took some heroin and began to drink heavily.

That's when it happened. For no apparent reason, someone walked up to me and stabbed me in the chest. I was so "stoned" that I didn't even know who had stabbed me—or why.

I staggered through the noisy crowd to the bathroom and vainly tried to stop the bleeding with paper towels. Weak and confused, I stumbled outside and collapsed in the gutter. *Everybody here knows me,* I thought, *but nobody cares.*

Suddenly a voice from the past arose from deep in my spirit. Years before, I had spurned an Anglican minister's offer to pray for me. Now his parting words pierced my heart: "Jesus still walks the streets today, and one day you are going to need Him. If you call on Him, He'll walk over to you and touch you."

Lying in the gutter with my life slipping away, I grabbed hold of those words. "Jesus," I cried, "if you're still waking the streets, come over to me now."

Jesus immediately responded to my pleas. At that moment a young Christian man picked me up, carried me to his car and drove me to the hospital. It was as if the hands and voice of God had been extended to me.

Three days later, when I regained consciousness in the hospital, this compassionate stranger was waiting for me. When I was released, he drove me home. There, he told me about his best friend, Jesus, and he led me in the sinner's prayer.

Through that experience, I learned the power of a prophetic word. I also realized the need for Christians to be God's voice to the world.

I believe the Lord wants to use every Christian the way he used those two men to turn my life around.

A PROPHET?

After I was converted, I wondered if God would—or could—ever use someone like me in the ministry. Yet He stirred within me a sense of calling. I didn't understand it but knew it was there.

After being rebuffed at every turn by those who doubted my calling, I prayed for a word from the Lord. At first I heard only a still, small voice. "I have called you to be a prophet to many nations," the Holy Spirit whispered in my heart.

"A prophet?" I asked the Lord. "You want *me* to be a prophet?"

I had hoped the Lord would say that He called me to use my musical talent for His glory. But every time I prayed, the voice grew louder and louder: "I have called you to be a prophet to many nations."

A prophet? I wondered. *Why would the Lord call me to be a prophet?*

But the Lord had spoken. And today I travel throughout the world building up the body of Christ through prophetic teaching and encouragement.

When God speaks, He creates something from nothing—something that was not there before. Why does He operate in this manner?

I believe it is so we cannot take the glory or credit for His handiwork. When the word of the Lord comes to pass, it's important that the world be compelled to say,

May 1994, Charisma

"That is the work of God, not man."

There is nothing to compare with God's creative word. Often when He speaks, He creates something inside us that we don't already possess.

I like to think of God's prophetic words as an outer shell that He allows to be filled and completed. Spiritual rebirth, for example, is only the beginning of our walk with Christ. We become new creations through the new birth so we can be "built together for a dwelling place of God in the Spirit" (see Eph. 2:22, NKJV).

That's the pattern: God first creates something, then completes and inhabits it.

A DOOR OF OPPORTUNITY

After years of ministering the prophetic word, this is how I have come to understand the role of prophecy: When the Lord speaks; it is as if a door of opportunity has been opened.

The prophetic word reveals the desire of God's heart for that person's life. But if that person refuses to walk through the door God has created for them, he or she will not see the revelation fulfilled.

Recently when I was conducting a service in Rhode Island, I noticed a young man in the audience. He sat with his arms crossed and was frowning. I could tell he was suffering from a disease that had disfigured his face.

Sensing that God wanted me to minister to the unconverted people in the crowd, I walked over to this young man. When I asked him to stand, he rose reluctantly. I could see he was extremely weak.

JUST AS WE ARE TO BE JESUS' HANDS AND FEET IN THE WORLD, WE ARE TO BE HIS VOICE.

Then God gave me a prophetic word concerning some specific things about his life.

"Sir," I said, "opportunity stands at your door. You have a choice. The Lord says: 'If you will turn to Me, I will raise you up, heal your bones and make you a man of God. You will live to tell the world of My glory and power.'"

That message clearly surprised the young man. When I spoke with some of his relatives after the meeting; they told me he had a rare type of bone cancer. Doctors had given him only months to live.

Members of his family had convinced him to

travel all the way from California to attend the meeting—even though they knew he wanted little to do with Jesus or the church. His relatives told me that all his past religious experiences had been disappointing.

An evangelist would have given an altar call for him. A person with the gift of healing would have laid hands on him for an instant miracle. But I was there to deliver a prophetic word from the Lord. Now it was up to him to accept or reject God's call to repent.

When this young man sat down, he was not suddenly free from the cancer. But he left the meeting with a new idea about who Jesus was. He realized that even in his pathetic state God was concerned enough to speak to him.

The next day the young man told his sister, "I need this Jesus the man was preaching about." As the two of them prayed together, he surrendered his heart to the Lord.

That night he attended the service again. He was a transformed man: His scowl was gone, and he was lifting his hands and celebrating his salvation—and his physical healing.

THE ROLE OF PROPHECY

Just as we are to be Jesus' hands and feet in the world, we are to be His voice. That, I believe, is the essence of prophecy: Through the power of the Holy Spirit we can communicate the voice of Christ to people around us.

I believe God desires the gift of prophecy to flow through millions of believers today. But in my understanding of the Scriptures, I believe the purpose of a prophet today is drastically different than it was in Old Testament times.

Under the old covenant—when the Holy Spirit had not yet been poured out on mankind—men like Jeremiah, Ezekiel and Isaiah often pronounced judgments on nations and predicted future events. Though on some occasions New Testament prophets might do those things, that is not their primary role.

Here are three important keys to understanding the role of prophecy under the new covenant:

1 Prophecy is for the church. The gift of prophecy is primarily intended to give direction to the body of Christ. Though God chose to bring a young man to Rhode Island to salvation through prophecy, Scripture tells us that "prophesying is not for unbelievers but for those who believe" (1 Cor. 14:22).

The gift of prophecy helps equip believers for ministry by revealing God's plans for the future (Acts

11:28), by providing unknown information about a situation (John 4:16–19), by disclosing the "secrets" of someone's heart (1 Cor. 14:24–25) or by providing knowledge of someone's gifts and callings (1 Tim. 1:18; 4:14).

When believers hear from God, they are equipped to bring unbelievers to Christ. That is God's plan. Because God speaks to the world through believers, it is vital that we not only hear but speak His word.

2 Prophecy is to be given in love. The moment you say, "Thus says the Lord," you are representing God through your speech. If He gives you the word, He will also let you know how He is feeling about the person to whom you are speaking.

In Old Testament times, when a ruler sent a message to another land, the spokesman would make every effort to deliver it in the same tone in which it was given to him. If his master felt great sorrow, that's what the messenger would express. If the king had laughed, his messenger would laugh too.

That same method needs to be used in prophetic ministry. The word God gives you must be spoken within the character and personality of Jesus. If not, the message will fail—no matter how accurate it is.

When Jesus talked with the woman at the well, he knew everything about her life. But He used great discretion in choosing His words. We, too, must speak compassionately. We should dismiss prophecies that are delivered in an indignant, condemning manner.

A prophetic minister must know more than what to say; he must know how to say it. Jesus said: "Behold, I send you out as sheep in the midst of wolves. Therefore be wise as serpents and harmless as doves" (Matt. 10:16).

3 Prophecy presents a promise of God. The prophetic ministry is a ministry of hope. It presents a divine revelation of God's dream for tomorrow.

When God speaks, He gives a remarkable preview of what His people can expect. He talks about today and tomorrow, not yesterday.

Rarely does a prophetic word tell you specific steps you must take to reach the goal, however. A prophecy simply tells you what God wants for your future. It is up to you to seek Him further about how to walk obediently in His plan.

If God says that He will do something, you may rest assured that's exactly what He intends to do. But there are conditions He requires on our part.

Scripture says: "Today, if you will hear His voice, do not harden your hearts" (Heb. 3:7–8). If we harden our hearts, today remains today and God's promise for tomorrow will never come. If we are to see the promise become a reality, we must accept it, believe it and wait patiently for Him to act.

GODS VOICE TO THE WORLD

When my son, Caleb, was a small baby, my wife and I would put him in the church nursery while I conducted services. As often happens when a child is in the presence of strangers, he became irritated and aggravated with the other children.

One night, at the end of a lengthy service, I saw someone bring my son into the rear of the auditorium. The moment he heard the sound of my voice, his entire disposition changed. He was instantly transformed from a miserable little lad into an excited, cheerful child.

My voice was familiar to Caleb. It was a sound that instinctively gave him comfort and security.

He didn't need to see me or even touch me. The sound of his father's voice was all he needed.

It is the same for each of us as children of God. If we will take the opportunity to hear our Father's voice, He will do great and marvelous things in our lives. He will not only give us insights into His plans for the future, but He will show us how to live now.

And as we grow familiar with the sound of His voice, we can share His life-changing words with a lost and dying world. If you are a member of the body of Christ and have received His Spirit, the breath of God resides in you. He has given you the ability to communicate for one great purpose: He wants to speak to the world through your voice.

Our natural reaction, of course, is to ask, "Why would God want to speak through me?" That was Moses' reaction when the Lord instructed him to challenge Pharaoh.

If we will but launch out in faith and ask, "Lord, what do you want me to say?" we can begin a great adventure with God that could bring many people into His kingdom.

—Kim Clement has taken his inspired message to schools, churches, synagogues, prison cells, the Rose Bowl Stadium in California, Times Square in New York City, Mt. Carmel in Israel, and even the steps of the U.S. Capitol in Washington, D.C. A native of South Africa, Kim Clement travels internationally as a prophetic minister. He is the author of Secrets of the Prophetic (Destiny Image Publishers).

Reprinted by permission: Charisma Magazine and Strang Communications Company.

May 1994, Charisma

GUIDELINES FOR THE PROPHETIC WORD

by Jeff King

Most of us who've been in or around Pentecostal and charismatic circles for any length of time have heard "prophetic words." We've been in meetings where a spontaneous message has been spoken by some leader or member of the congregation, prefaced by "Thus saith the Lord." At one time or another we've had someone approach us saying, The Lord has given me a word for you."

Perhaps some of us have been the voice of such messages—and have sensed the Lord speaking to us and through us about specific matters of our own lives and the lives of others.

Such experiences can bring great encouragement and strength to both the recipient and the giver.

They can also become a source of confusion and frustration in the church.

Every church leader must grapple with certain questions regarding prophetic words. For example, are we to assume that every "Thus saith the Lord" spoken by every believer in every setting is a word form God? Should we accept all prophetic messages without question?

What if we sense something is amiss in what we hear? How can we discern between what is truly from God and what originates from other sources?

And what about those who give the messages? To what guidelines and responsibilities do they submit themselves? What kind of precautions do we need to take to ensure that we speak accurately when giving a word inspired by God?

These questions deserve careful consideration as we strive to preserve the integrity and blessing of God's gifts to His people. For indeed, true prophecy and prophetic words are biblically based manifestations of the gifts of the Holy Spirit (see 1 Cor. 12:4–11).

As such, these messages fall under the guidelines given in Scripture to govern the use of spiritual gifts. Many problems and excesses with administering prophetic words have undoubtedly arisen because of our all-too-human tendency to resist the discipline and boundaries that must accompany God-given privilege and power.

RECEIVING A PROPHECY

1 Thessalonians 5:19–21 emphasizes a balanced approach in response to a prophetic word. We are instructed not to quench the Holy Spirit by despising the prophetic message. In other words, we are not to let a cynical or overly suspicious attitude cause us to deny the possibility of this type of communication from the Holy Spirit.

Some err on the "suspicious" side, overreacting to past experiences in which the prophetic gift was mishandled. Yet adopting such a posture keeps us from the blessings that are intended by God in the legitimate use of prophecy.

Scripture records many occasions where this gift was used to accomplish the work of God. In the Old Testament, for example, the prophet Nathan exercised the gift to expose David's sin (2 Sam. 12:1–15). And in the New Testament a prophetic word gave Paul and Barnabas direction for their first missionary journey (see Acts 13:1–3).

These legitimate uses fulfilled God's intention for the prophetic gift: to "speak to men for edification and exhortation and consolation" (1 Cor. 14:3). Many today can testify of the usefulness and timeliness of this gift of the Spirit. They have received encouragement, strength and direction to carry out God's will for their lives.

Unfortunately, there are also those who have suffered as a result of the misuse of this gift, hence the second portion of the exhortation to the Thessalonians. We are not to receive such messages blindly without carefully evaluating them—a warning that implies not everything preceded with "Thus saith the Lord" is from God.

To evaluate a prophetic message, we must ask:

- *Does the message line up with God's written Word?* If a message goes against what is written or breaks from principles set forth in the Scriptures, it must be rejected.
- *Does it confirm previously revealed direction from the Lord?* In Paul and Barnabas' situation, the prophetic message provided additional guidance for the mission God already had established for their lives. People should never make a crucial lifestyle change (getting married, going on a missionary adventure, quitting a job, etc.) solely on the basis of a prophetic word. The Bible makes clear that God's children are led by the Holy Spirit (Rom. 8:14), not by isolated "personal prophecies."
- *Is the content accurate?* Does it agree with known facts of the situation?

Such questions are considered to be "unspiritual" by some, and often the message is spoken with such fervency that the recipient is afraid to ask them. The result is confusion when the receiver knows the content has inconsistencies or doesn't apply to his situation.

GIVING A PROPHETIC WORD

These principles should also serve notice to the one giving a prophecy to examine carefully the message and the motive behind it. As we see in 1 Corinthians 14:29–33, the human element plays an important role in prophecy.

While exercising this gift, therefore, we need to examine ourselves honestly. Are we expressing God's thoughts—or is there a possibility the message is merely our own agenda coming out as an oracle from God?

Sometimes we are tempted to promote our own desires, opinions, and causes under the guise of "a word from the Lord." This is a particular danger when we have become frustrated, angry, or discontented with our church or those around us.

It is also a hazard when we have become strongly impassioned with a particular truth, cause or experience. At such times we can lose our sense of balance and objectivity and use prophecy as a platform to voice our convictions.

Similarly, we can fall into the trap of using prophecy as a way to manipulate and coerce others. Some have suffered spiritual abuse from those who have attempted to control them under the veneer of prophecy.

In addition to evaluating our motives for giving a prophetic word, we must examine the content of the message. Not only must we be concerned with accuracy in facts and figures, we must also guard against meaningless repetition and vagueness.

Some "prophecies" end up sounding suspiciously alike, with many of the main terms repeated over and over. Based on past experiences with the speaker, listeners sometimes can predict what will be said and how it will be stated!

We must ask ourselves: Is this message a timely word for those present? Or is it a repetition of spiritual-sounding jargon, vague promises and empty exhortations? Do I have a word from the Lord that will benefit the hearers, or am I merely overcome with spiritual excitement?

AVOIDING ERROR

The need to evaluate prophecy at both the giving and receiving ends makes additional guidelines necessary. Their importance is evident when we observe some common errors in the exercise of the prophetic gift.

1 **Hear what God is saying—not what you want Him to say.** One danger to receivers is the tendency to make a prophecy say what we want to hear. When prophetic words are general or vague, this is simple enough to do. By nature, such words leave the interpretation solely up to the hearer.

We need to be particularly careful in cases where we have strong desires toward a particular course of action. We must guard against twisting such a prophecy to justify what we already plan on doing, remaining just as open to hearing God say "No" as "Yes."

2 **Don't become dependent on personal prophecy.** We must guard against becoming dependent upon others, especially a particular individual, to have a word for us. God's plan for revealing Himself is to plant the Holy Spirit within each of us and give us His written Word for study.

He does not want us to become dependent upon others for guidance. Erring this way, many people in effect have adopted their own personal "seers." This borders on divination and spiritism —and it's dangerous.

A word of warning must go to the giver of personal prophecies as well. We must refrain from allowing others to attach themselves to us in this manner and resist the temptation to adopt the position of power and influence that such a relationship brings

3 **Don't be flippant with the phrase, "Thus saith the Lord."** With frequency comes familiarity—making it all too easy to develop a sense of carelessness or even arrogance in making the claim, "God told me…" With overuse, we tend to lose the reverence and impact that such a statement demands and deserves.

4 **Make yourself accountable.** 1 Corinthians 14:29 instructs us to submit our message to others for their evaluation and discernment. We are called to be accountable to others (specifically to leadership) with the content and motives of our prophetic messages.

This is not popular in some circles today, where self-proclaimed "prophets" operate with little or no accountability. They assert that they speak for God but are reluctant to submit their messages for evaluation. Many errors would be avoided if only this one directive were closely followed!

Furthermore, some use prophecy as grounds for becoming aloof and separated from the church and its accountability structure. How often in recent years have we known or heard of people who've chose not to follow the rest of the church in a particular activity or direction because "the Lord told them" not to do so!

The truth more often than not, is that they do not want to participate, submit, or otherwise fulfill their responsibility as a member of the body. Proverbs 18:1 warns against such practices.

ADDRESSING PROPHETIC CONFUSION

What should we do if someone conveys a prophetic word that falls into one of these errors? What if the word does not bear witness with our spirit, leaving us and others confused? Depending on the nature of the word and the circumstances surrounding it, a variety of responses are scripturally appropriate.

One is the direct approach. If we have a good rapport with the one giving the word, or if it has been given in a public meeting where many are in danger of confusion, a gentle confrontation that focuses on the error is entirely in order.

Specific scriptures or biblical principles should be cited to help ensure the instruction and benefit of all involved. Care should be taken not to demean or discourage the giver from continuing to seek to be used by the Lord in the spiritual gifts.

In public situations, this correction is the responsibility of the pastor or recognized leader of the group. Responsibility rests on the giver, as well, to have a teachable attitude, realizing that he or she is not above the possibility of error.

In more private situations where the message is ambiguous or confusing, it is fitting to ask the giver for clarification. For example, the giver could be asked how he or she would interpret or apply the message—thus making room to clear up any misunderstanding. Again, this should be done with a Christ-like attitude on both sides, free from accusation, judgmentalism and defensiveness.

Sometimes, however, the best response to prophecy is that of Mary, who received many prophetic messages about Jesus. In Luke 2:51 it says that she "treasured all these things in her heart."

Some questions about a prophecy do not merit a direct confrontation, and it may not be possible or beneficial to dialogue about it. Time can be the best test for prophecy, particularly in these instances. It gives us an opportunity to think, pray, get counsel from mature believers and wait for any further revelation concerning the message.

Ultimately, our biblical response to the prophetic word is to maintain balance. We are not to despise prophecy; we are to welcome and purse it.

Yet in doing so, we must use wisdom and discernment, guarding against the excesses and misuses of our fallen state. When we follow the biblical pattern, we experience the blessings of the prophetic word that God intended—the edification, exhortation and consolation that come from God speaking to me, through men, by the power of the Holy Spirit.

—Jeff King has served as Pastor of Family Ministries and Pastoral Care at the Community Covenant Church in Osage City, Kansas.

THE GIFT OF PROPHECY

by John Wimber

PERSONAL REVELATIONS ARE BIBLICAL AND PROFITABLE, BUT WE MUST BE VIGILANT IN TESTING THEM AGAINST SCRIPTURAL GUIDELINES.

The Bible teaches that God communicates with us in a variety of ways. For example, God speaks in a general way to all men and women through creation (Ps. 19:1–2), through our consciences (Rom. 2:14–15) and through His continuing providence (Acts 14:17). He communicates more directly through the written Word, which is not only the written record of His acts, but also the authoritative revelation of who He is and how we may have communion with Him.

But it does not end there. In the Old and New Testaments, we see God speaking to His children in dramatic, sometimes startling ways: prophecies, dreams and visions, inner impressions, angels, tongues and interpretations, among others.

The gift of prophecy, mentioned by the apostle Paul in 1 Corinthians 12:10, is one method of God's communication that is receiving a great deal of emphasis in the contemporary church. Unfortunately, there has been neglect, misunderstanding or misuse of this manifestation of the Spirit—everywhere from Corinth to California, and from the first century to the 20th.

At the heart of the debate over contemporary prophecy is the question, How can we know if we are hearing from God?

NOW HEAR THIS

The apostle Paul says that if an unbeliever comes into the church when people are prophesying, he or she may be convinced they are telling the truth and may discover God there (1 Cor. 14:24-25). In our own Vineyard

Christian Fellowship in Anaheim, California, this has happened repeatedly. Not long ago, a church member approached a female visitor and told her the secrets of her heart. As a result, the woman knew God was speaking to her, was converted and is now happily settled in our church.

Such a prophetic word is not a prepared message or a learned skill. Nor should it be considered to have the same authority as Scripture. It's simply an immediate report of some revelation the Spirit has given in regard to a contemporary situation (1 Cor. 14:29–30).

The gift of prophecy is generally a message of strengthening, encouragement and comfort (14:3). It's an inspired message for the moment in the common language and could be prefaced by "Now hear this."

Unfortunately, the idea that God can and does speak to us in such a way frightens some Christians because it involves subjective experience. They readily accept preaching, teaching, witnessing and Bible study as authentic ways God speaks because they appear to be so clearly rooted in Scripture. Yet even these "objective" means of revelation are affected by the more subjective element of the Spirit's quickening the hearts of both the speaker and hearers. And while all Christians agree with the authority of Scripture, not all agree with how to interpret it.

Some Christians even maintain that belief in more subjective expressions of God's communication opens the door to emotional delusion or, worse yet, satanic deception. Fearing the worst, they retreat to the position that the Bible is the *sole* source of revelation today. (Their position is not that God *could not* speak today in

November 1992, Charisma

these ways, but that He has chosen not to.)

But are their concerns actually rooted in the teaching of Scripture? Or is their interpretation based more on their anxieties or bad experiences?

The most casual reading of the Bible teaches that in biblical times God spoke to His people through the prophetic gifts. The Bible also teaches that He will speak to us in a similar way even today.

But how do we avoid the pitfalls of subjective revelation? How can we know if a prophetic message is truly from God? If prophecy, dreams, visions and other forms of direct revelation are biblical, then it's reasonable to look for biblical guidelines regarding their authenticity.

GUIDELINES

What safe guards, then, does Scripture provide to ensure that we are not led astray by "prophetic" words?

1. Personal prophecy should glorify the Word of God, Jesus Christ. The Holy Spirit's primary mission is to bring glory to the Son (John 16:14), so any prophecy dream or vision should point us toward Jesus.

A good test for knowing if we are crossing the line on this point is to ask two questions:

- Does the prophetic person often talk about himself (or herself). Subtly lifting up his experience and ministry at the expense of Jesus' glory? If so, we will have an uncomfortable feeling, getting more caught up in his or her story than in the life of Christ.

THE CONTENT OF EXTRA-BIBLICAL REVELATION SHOULD ALWAYS BE IN ACCORDANCE WITH AND SUBMITTED TO SCRIPTURE.

- Are we constantly seeking after and hoping for words from the prophetic person, so much so that we suffer disappointment and even depression when we don't receive one? Then he or she is undermining out ability to hear from God through His Word and through the "still small voice" of the Holy Spirit.

2. Prophetic messages should conform to the Word of God, the Bible. Paul says elders must "encourage others by sound doctrine and refute those who oppose it" (Tit. 1:9, NIV). The content of extra-biblical revelation

should always be in accordance with and submitted to Scripture. A so-called "word" that encourages someone to commit adultery or to believe that Jesus was *not* raised from the dead is rejected because it is a direct refutation of Scripture.

Some personal words of prophecy, however, deal with issues not addressed by the Bible. Those revelations that can be neither contradicted nor verified by Scripture should not be rejected out of hand. For example, prophetic words that warn someone about a dangerous business dealing or a hurtful relationship may or may not be legitimate. There are other criteria for judging their authenticity.

3. Prophecy should not be used to establish doctrine or practice. This is more subtle than the previous point.

The apostle Paul warned Timothy about anyone who "teaches false doctrine and does not agree to the sound instruction of our Lord Jesus Christ and to godly teaching" (1 Tim. 6:3). In that day as this, some experiences and so called revelations are outside the scope of both Scripture and everyday experience, and thus should not be looked to as authoritative truth for understanding major doctrine and practice. In other words, private prophecy can never control our interpretation of Scripture.

I've observed that Christians don't always recognize when prophetically gifted people are allowing private revelations to control their understanding of Scripture. After hearing remarkable and accurate prophetic words, for example, it's easy to lower our guards and not think biblically when a prophetic person begins teaching from the Bible.

We are dazzled by their prophetic gifts and blinded to their biblical ignorance. If they are so right about all the details of my life, we think, how could they be wrong about Scripture? This is especially a temptation when a prophetic minister speaks about doctrines surrounding the second coming of Christ, a subject rife with speculation about which church leaders have never been in agreement.

We must resist the temptation to allow a "private revelation" to overcome the most basic principles of biblical interpretation. Scripture, not prophecy, is the ultimate test of all doctrine and practice.

4. Those who deliver a prophetic word should be of sound moral character, submitted to the lordship of Jesus and producing good fruit in their ministry.

Jesus warned that false prophets would come in "sheep's clothing" (Matt. 7:15–23), meaning they would be camouflaged to look like one of us. So how are we to

November 1992, Charisma

know the difference between a true and a false prophet?

Jesus said we are to be fruit inspectors: "By their fruit you will recognize them" (Matt. 7:16). Does their ministry point people to Jesus and His Word? Are folks led to repentance and deeper faith in God?

This means that a person delivering prophecies should be willing to have his or her words tested by the elders of the church (1 Cor. 14:29–32). Pastoral oversight tests prophetic ministry and guides its recipients in appropriate responses. Complaints or questions about specific prophetic ministry should be thoroughly investigated and brought to clear resolution by responsible pastors.

If a prophetic word predicts a future event, it should be fulfilled. If the predicted event does not happen, either God has not spoken (Deut. 18:21–22), or unspoken conditions of the prophecy were not fulfilled (Jer. 18:7–10; Jon. 2–4).

The quality of a person's fruit is determined by his or her character. A good test of mature character is to see if the messenger is submitted to pastoral oversight. Independent, unteachable and self-proclaimed "prophets" are dangerous. To protect the body of Christ, the pastors and elders of a congregation should check out the character and fruit of anyone who prophesies. A failure to do this leads to all kinds of abuse and hurt in the body of Christ.

The problem of independent, traveling people who stir up significant pastoral problems in congregations is not confined to the prophetic. The phenomenon of traveling teachers, evangelists and self-styled apostles who abuse Christians and cause controversy and division is widespread. In this regard, independent prophetic figures are only a part of the bigger problem of hyper-individualism in Western Christianity and the unwillingness of pastors to give proper oversight to their ministry.

5. Prophetic messages should be given in the spirit of love (1 Cor. 14:3, James 3:17). Even a word of rebuke is to be given in the spirit of love. Information about individuals that is negative or that may be embarrassing should not be spoken publicly without first confronting the individual in private.

> MANY PERSONAL PROPHETIC WORDS GIVEN TODAY ARE INVITATIONS — NOT CERTAINTIES.

Prophetic gifting should never be used for controlling purposes. It should be overseen to ensure that believers' personal responsibility and authority for their own lives (as well as pastoral authority over a church) are not undermined.

6. No one should make major decisions based on personal prophetic words alone (1 Cor. 14:27–32). Personal prophetic words should be weighed by elders, pastors and other prophetic people, as well as the person who is receiving the word. Personal words should be given in a way and in a setting that allows for this to happen.

For example, the prophet Agabus warned Paul that if he went to Jerusalem, he would be arrested, and the other disciples pleaded with him not to go (Acts 21:10–14). Paul accepted the prophetic word but still went on to Jerusalem, where he was later arrested. He accepted the revelation of his coming suffering, but he rejected the disciples' application—that he therefore should not go.

A friend of mine recently told me of a simultaneous dream that he and his wife experienced one night last March. The dreams were almost identical, with the exception of a few details. The dreams came at a time when they were deciding among several job opportunities. The dream seemed to indicate he should reject a job that, by most other criteria, he should accept. When he approached a prophetically gifted person, he was told the interpretation was "obvious" —he should not accept the job he thought was for him.

"But," he told me, "the older I get, the less I trust 'obvious' answers." So he and his wife instead trusted the quiet leading of the Holy Spirit. They took the job that the prophetic person warned them about, and decided to wait and see if there was another interpretation to their dreams. Six months later, a series of events occurred that gave an entirely different—and accurate—understanding to their dreams. Had he relied on the "prophetic" insight into their dreams, they would have missed out on God's call for their lives.

7. Many, if not most personal prophetic words given today are conditional and, as such, are invitations — not certainties (Jer. 18:7–10). We must continue to seek God for the promised blessings to come to pass.

I'm a little uncomfortable whenever I teach this point because it can be construed as an easy out for missed prophecy. "The prophet wasn't wrong," we hear. "The disobedience of the person who received the prophecy prevented the word from being fulfilled." This argument is similar to the one that blames any lack of healing on the paltry faith of the person being prayed for.

November 1992, Charisma

The problem with this thinking, though, is that the primary responsibility for healing in Scripture is laid at the feet of the person who prays, not on the sick. Likewise, in the majority of instances where a prophetic word is unfulfilled, it should be attributed to inaccurate prophecy, not disobedience on the receiver's part.

The gift of prophecy and other personal revelations must be received and understood in a biblical way. And we must be vigilant in testing all that we believe and do against Scripture.

If we do that, our lives will fulfill Paul's prayer in Philippians 1:9–11: "That your love may abound more and more in knowledge and depth of insight, so that you may be able to discern what is best and may be pure and blameless until the day of Christ, filled with the fruit of righteousness that comes through Jesus Christ—to the glory and praise of God."

—John Wimber (1934-1997) was a founding leader of the Vineyard community of churches and author of books on healing and evangelism.

Reprinted by permission: Charisma Magazine and Strang Communications Company.

ASSIGNED ARTICLE

TONGUES AND INTERPRETATION

by Jack Hayford

THE PUBLIC AND CORPORATE EXERCISE OF THESE GIFTS ACCOMPLISHES A GREAT WORK WHEN THEY ARE SENSITIVELY AND SCRIPTURALLY EXERCISED.

Few issues provoke more debate in Christian circles today than spiritual gifts —their validity, their use, their abuse. There's no debate, however, as to which of the nine gifts of the Holy Spirit raise the most question or opposition. The gift of tongues and its companion gift of interpretation are so often misunderstood and so frequently misapplied that it's no surprise they are often called "the least of the gifts."

That phrase is used with such frequency—usually to demean speaking in tongues—that we might be inclined to presume the words "least of the gifts" must be somewhere in the Bible. But they aren't.

None of the precious gifts of God's Spirit – tongues included – should *ever* be deemed "less than the rest." The gifts are all from Him – the sovereign Spirit, who distributes them at *His* will. Their Source should forever preclude us from placing a diminishing value on any of the gifts, as though the order of their listing indicated a divine preference. (If that were true, "faith, hope and love" are listed in the wrong order in 1 Corinthians 13:13 because the last on the list is named "the greatest"!)

Nevertheless, there are biblical grounds for designating "the best gifts" (1 Cor. 12:31). The "best gift," quite simply, is the one most suited to a given situation. When the apostle Paul exhorts us to "earnestly desire the best," he isn't setting up a competition, but he is urging us to be open to the full and free working of the Holy Spirit.

In the atmosphere of *love* (1 Cor. 13), the diversity of the Spirit's *gifts* (1 Cor. 12) will *edify the church* (1 Cor. 14). These three chapters in 1 Corinthians converge to point the way toward the best thing (edification) being accomplished the best way (love) by the Holy Spirit manifesting the best gift—the most appropriate gift to answer the need in any given situation. Since sometimes the best gift may be tongues, where do tongues and interpretations fit in?

It shouldn't surprise us that we have questions about the proper use of tongues and interpretation today. After all, even in the pristine environment of the first-century church, confusion over the exercise of these gifts necessitated Paul's corrective and discerning instruction to the Corinthians. Almost 2,000 years later, it is encouraging to find tongues and interpretation alive and operating at all, given the number of people who would drum them out of the church. The fact is, tongues and interpretation are not only worthy as gifts, but they also accomplish a great work when they are sensitively and scripturally welcomed and exercised.

How can the gifts of "different kinds of tongues" and "the interpretation of tongues" be best understood and responded to by today's Spirit-filled Christian? Just as we have the "three R's" in education, let me suggest "three R's" for edification through these gifts: realm, regulation and release.

THE REALM

To say these gifts function in the spiritual realm seems so obvious as to be unnecessary for comment. But we need to start here for two reasons. First, because it explains the essence of these gifts, and second, because it will guide us regarding their substance.

We find in 1 Corinthians 14:3 that the essence

June 1993, Charisma

of tongues and interpretation is to bring an idea from God—a coherent set of words, intended to build up (edify), stir up (exhort) or lift up (comfort). This is a complex accomplishment: We are dealing with the desire of the infinite, all-knowing, all-wise Spirit to convey His mind, heart and purpose to a specific person or group at a distinct moment and on a select theme.

Remember the elaborate effort that went into employing the memorable five-tone message in *Close Encounters of a Third Kind*? A flawed illustration, perhaps, but it serves to remind us that we are dealing with an effort of the divine mind of God to express something to mere human understanding.

The miracle of the gift of tongues, functioning in tandem with interpretations of tongues, is that God has ordained them as a beautiful means for bridging the chasm between our finite minds and His infinite mind, calling our attention to something the Holy Spirit wants us to remember, understand or heed.

It is this "specific reminder" aspect that distinguishes tongues and interpretation from equivalency with the eternal Scriptures—the Bible. Everything we need to know about the Lord, His truth or its bearing on our lives is already contained in the Word of God. But messages in tongues and interpretation are pointed at a moment in our life to bring a direct message to our immediate circumstance.

The essence of this manifestation of the Holy Spirit is to get our attention in a supernatural way (the "tongue" has a way of doing that) and to speak a "word" from God's heart to ours. First Corinthians 14:5 says "a tongue," when interpreted, has purpose or value like a prophetic word. Such words will not only contain frequent references to the Scriptures, but they will *always* align with biblical truth. They also will usually draw our attention to a place in God's Word from which we may more fully feed on His intent for us for that moment.

And therein lies the substance—the durable, lasting "stuff" of a tongue and interpretation working in tandem. The essence of these gifts is to communicate from God to His people; the substance is to focus His heart's concern for us at the present moment by ultimately getting us into and in alignment with His Word.

THE REGULATIONS

First Corinthians 14 is full of guidelines for the exercise of these two gifts, along with the gift of prophecy. But these rules are subject to interpretation; thus, anyone is vulnerable to criticism if he or she seems to tread on an approach held sacrosanct by a group holding a differing opinion. Still, I have identified a foundational set of principles regulating tongues and interpretation that seems to be broadly acknowledged throughout the body of Christ worldwide.

1. They are to be commonly expected. The bible indicates that "a tongue…an interpretation"(1 Cor. 14:26) will be a rather regular occurrence at gatherings of believers. Nothing suggests a meeting is "more spiritual" for this having occurred, nor is it a requirement—because the distribution of gifts is not ours to dictate (1 Cor. 12:11). But there may be reason for concern if this manifestation gradually disappears from a group.

I know I periodically feel the need to prompt our leaders to "stir up" this and other gifts (2 Tim. 1:6)—not that we initiate or instigate what the Holy Spirit alone directs, but that we keep our hearts open to His readiness to manifest Himself through the gifts (1 Cor. 12:7).

2. They are to be controlled. The human element in responding to the Holy Spirit's prompting is clearly stated in 1 Corinthians 14. The number of "messages in tongues' should not exceed three (v. 27). A tongue should not be brought unless an interpretation is sure to be forthcoming (v. 28). Messages given by this means are subject to evaluation and correction in the light of the Scriptures (v. 29). No one has the right to claim, "I simply had to say it; the Spirit made me do it," thus avoiding responsibility for either content or tastelessness in timing (vv. 30–32).

The exercise of such gifts should blend into a meeting to avoid confusion (v. 33) and submit to a basic beauty in the order of the gathering (v. 40). The word *euschemonos*—"decent" (NKJV), "fitting" (NIV) —is a clear call for the conduct of services in which the whole, including the manifestation of the Spirit's gifts, is both winsome and beautiful. God is not a God of disorder but of peace (v. 33, emphasis added).

These regulations are not intended to suffocate or suppress the operation of God's gifts, but rather to require their exercise in a mood and with a tone of divine dignity, unpolluted by human ignorance or arrogance. Sadly, some charismatic services are characterized by a casual indifference to these directives—often because the people are either untrained or have been inadvertently schooled by bad examples. Yet the Scriptures give us clear reasons for correcting such things as:

- Blatant, machine-gun delivery of verbal gifts in an interruptive way, at indiscriminate times in a service, or at a decibel level threatening to shatter the chandeliers
- Wandering "words" that drift on interminably, devoid of clarity or so casual in delivery as to suggest that "God just dropped in to have a chat"

June 1993, Charisma

- "Words" delivered in King James English, in an apparent attempt to confirm the inspiration level of the speaker
- Redundancy, when the same people in a congregation always seem "to bring *their* word" (a repetitious theme that usually is their message, not the Holy Spirit's)

3. They are to be released. The risk that any or all of these problems might occur is always present in a service open to the gifts of tongues and interpretation. This fact, however, should not discourage us from warmly welcoming their proper function.

Paul's intent is obvious in 1 Corinthians. He wants to avoid the confusion of the private, personal exercise of tongues (for prayer and praise) with the public, corporate exercise of tongues with interpretation (for edification of the body).

Paul insists on tastefulness and biblical order in the conduct of the gatherings of believers. In this regard, his final directives are (1) don't prohibit tongues (1 Cor. 14:39), and (2) don't despise prophecies (1 Thess. 5:20), which includes tongues with interpretation.

THE RELEASE

Books could be written to illustrate all the ways by which spiritually sensitive and biblically faithful leaders have led their congregations to a profitable responsiveness to the manifestations of the Holy Spirit. For the purpose of this brief overview, however, let me suggest three keys to maximizing the benefits of the exercise of tongues with interpretation in the body life of an assembly – and to reducing the liabilities of abuse.

1. Conviction. These gifts will not be manifest in an assembly where the leader is unconvinced of their importance for the body. No two gifts are more frequently explained away than these, often with rather inadequate excuses:
- "Tongues are only for praise."
- "A mature body outgrows tongues and interpretation and only exercises prophecy."
- "We don't like people saying, 'Thus saith the Lord.' It seems presumptuous."

All of these rationales indicate excuses and seem born of a lack of conviction as to the desirability of these two gifts. Yet all the gifts have been given to the church for our edification. Our challenge is to welcome all these gifts as the Spirit helps us grow in the grace of receiving them and to find out how to respond with God-honoring good sense. Any disposition to selectively pre-empt or snobbishly prefer what some consider "the best" gifts must be confronted.

THE ESSENCE OF TONGUES AND INTERPRETATION IS TO BRING AN IDEA FROM GOD—A COHERENT SET OF WORDS INTENDED TO BUILD UP (EDIFY), STIR UP (EXHORT) OR LIFT UP (COMFORT).

2. Instruction. We need to teach our congregations how to function in the gifts of the Holy Spirit. First, we need to see the nine gifts He gives as distinct from other categories of divine giftings, and teach on them specifically. Further, we need to remember that each of the nine has multiple ways of manifesting. (For example, I have not even begun to deal with the private or one-to-one exercise of tongues with interpretation in this article, but only with the public and corporate exercise of these two gifts.)

Second, Christians who are open to be used by the Holy Spirit in these ways deserve to be assisted in their understanding of how He prompts us toward exercising them. In our congregation, we have special "Gifts and Ministries" classes. These aren't to teach "how to perform" or "how to get God to do things." Rather, they teach biblical principles, explaining what believers might expect when the Spirit of God wants to distribute a spiritual gift through them for the blessing of an individual or the congregation.

3. Administration. Control of the operation of the verbal gifts of the Holy Spirit should never be viewed as a device for suppression. Yet a certain degree of control is essential—self-control, first of all, along with the administrative wisdom of the pastoral leaders of a congregation.

Many charismatics are too fearful of oppressive leaders (due to past pain) or too ferociously independent (due to a need to assert self-authority) to submit to such control. That may always be the case to some degree in the church at large. But the fullest, most effective release of the gifts of tongues and interpretation in a congregation will occur where specific administrative guidelines are taught and observed.

Effective administration involves both "urging people toward" and "cautioning people about" spiritual gifts. It involves local decisions as to how and when verbal gifts will manifest in public services—not restricting

June 1993, Charisma

them, but finding the best way to release their manifestation in beauty and order.

Tongues and interpretation may be last on the list of the nine gifts of the Holy Spirit, but they are not to be minimized or prioritized as "least." The believer and the assembly that learns to welcome them will inevitably be edified and blessed by these precious gifts—which are but another expression of our God's bounty toward us all.

—Jack Hayford is a Pentecostal minister, the founding pastor of Church on the Way in Van Nuys, California and Chancellor of The King's University. He was the fourth President of the International Church of the Four Square Gospel and is a prolific author and interdenominational church leader.

Reprinted by permission Charisma Magazine and Strang Communications Company.

ZOE COURSE DESCRIPTIONS

"My sheep <u>hear</u> My voice, and I <u>know</u> them, and they <u>follow</u> Me." John 10:27 (KJV)

HEARING COURSES

Hearing God's Voice

In this course, everyone is encouraged to participate by applying the principles they read in scripture in order to learn to recognize when the Holy Spirit is speaking. The inner knowing, inner voice, and the authoritative voice of the Holy Spirit are discussed, as well as other manifestations of the Holy Spirit. The Lord is personal and unique, and desires to communicate with each one of His sheep in a personal and unique manner! (This course is a prerequisite for all the following courses except for How to Hear God's Voice —In Marriage.)

How To Hear God's Voice—In Christ

In the Hearing God's Voice course we learned how to hear God as individuals, whereas in the In Christ course, we learn how the body of Christ operates together under His direction and to His glory. We look at Romans 12 and examine the motive gifts that determine our individual bents. This study enables us to understand, appreciate and love each other. We also look at the Trinity and how they operate together. We learn about the precious person of the Holy Spirit and how He teaches, guides and comforts us. We also learn about the gifts of the Holy Spirit in 1 Corinthians 12 and 14 brought about as the Holy Spirit moves through us. Participants have remarked that this course has enabled them to see people the way God sees them and how they fit in the body of Christ.

How To Hear God's Voice—In Marriage

This course is based on the love relationship God had with mankind in the very beginning. We examine our attitudes toward each other and how they reflect the greatest love of all, the love of Christ. Do we love and honor each other with the unconditional love that our Lord Jesus had for us while dying on the cross? As in previous courses, we examine scripture, seek the Lord, and ask Him, "How can I better serve and love my spouse?" We discover how we complete each other, not compete with each other.

How To Hear God's Voice—In the Family

In today's society we see the growing deterioration of the family. Parents are confused about what the Bible teaches on family issues. During this course we examine scriptures and what it means to: "Train up a child [early childhood] in the way he should go [and in keeping with his individual bent], and when he is old [teen years can be the best] he will not depart from it." (AMP with additions)

KNOWING COURSES

How To Know God's Voice—In Intimate Friendship

Intimate Friendship with God! Can we experience such a relationship with the Creator of the universe? Here we examine what the Bible teaches us about the fear of the Lord, and how we can, indeed, have a deeper, more intimate relationship with Him. This is a very personal, yet freeing course on growing intimacy with God.

How To Know God's Voice—In Worship

The focus of this course is on ministering to the Lord. During our time together the Lord draws us corporately into His presence as we worship Him. We study what worship is, why we worship, and how we worship.

How To Know God's Voice—In His Presence

The Lord is calling each one of His sheep to come into His presence and to know Him in a deeper way. This course is not for the new believer nor the faint in heart. Those who are serious about knowing the Father in a more intimate way will find this course challenging but rewarding. Examining Jesus' last days on earth will direct us into the presence of the Lord. This course is for those who have completed other ZOE courses.

IIow To Know God's Voice—In the Coming of the Lord

Many are proclaiming dates and times when the Lord Jesus will return for His bride. This course is designed to focus on our preparation for His coming, not when He is coming, and to better understand the Lord's statement of Revelation 22:20: "Yes, I am coming." It is the goal of this course to prepare ourselves as the bride of Christ, with hearts that will respond with "Amen. Come, Lord Jesus."

FOLLOWING COURSES

How To Follow God's Voice—In Power

Once we have learned how to hear God's voice and we walk in intimate friendship with Jesus, don't we want to go out and share with others what Jesus has done for us? In this course, Following God's Voice - In Power we come to realize that God has a special plan for evangelism for us if only we are sensitive and obedient to His voice. Preparing your testimony, leading someone in salvation, and discipling others are a few of the topics discussed in this course. This is a real life-changer as we minister in "power evangelism"!

How To Follow God's Voice—In Healing

During this course we examine the scriptures in which Jesus healed the sick. The Holy Spirit highlights these passages as we study, and our faith increases! We realize that Jesus is the Healer, and we are simply His vessels as we listen to and follow His voice.

How To Follow God's Voice—In Intercession

In this course we study Scriptures about intercession, and we learn to ask God how to pray for each specific prayer request. We ask Him, "How can we see Your hand at work in this situation? Guide us as we pray." God is faithful to lead us in prayer as we seek His direction. Most people don't like to pray. But when you pray with God's heart, direction and the leading of the Holy Spirit, prayer becomes exciting.

How To Follow God's Voice—In Spiritual Warfare

When we accept Christ as our Lord and Savior, we are automatically enlisted in His army. Through Christ we have been given authority and power with which to deal with the enemy. In this course we learn our position in Christ (Ephesians 2:6) and whom we are actually fighting (Ephesians 6:12). We will be victorious as we remember our authority in Christ, rather than focusing on Satan.

ONE-ON-ONE DISCIPLESHIP

Discipleship. . . By the Word of God and the Power of the Holy Spirit

This 12-week course was developed by a disciple-maker after many years of successful one-on-one discipleship. Through this method the Holy Spirit is allowed to minister to the disciple through the Word and the encouragement of the disciple-maker. No other techniques or methods are used.

The entire course has been designed to enable individuals to feel confident in making disciples as directed by our Lord: *"Therefore go and make disciples of all nations …."* Matthew 28:19

Not only do the participants learn what discipleship means according to the Word of God, but they are encouraged to participate in a one-on-one discipleship program as part of the course. This training allows individuals to take great strides in their personal relationship with God and in ministry. It changes lives in a very simple, yet powerful way.

EVANGELISTIC OUTREACH — MINISTRY IN HOMES

Captivated by Their Character

This series of courses called Captivated by Their Character is designed to reach the unbeliever, new believer, and those needing a refresher course on the Trinity.

They are offered in a non-threatening, home atmosphere where every effort is made to make the participant feel comfortable with the material. For example, everyone uses the same Bible, referring to page numbers rather than books, no reading is required outside of the course, and they are given the freedom to express their inadequacies as a believer or non-believer.

Additional information is available on the website at www.zoeministries.org/zoe-courses

Following this page you will find:

Summary of the Motive Gifts, ZOE Ministries

This article is provided as supplementary reading. It summarizes much of the information presented in class about each motive gift.

How To Hear God's Voice—In Christ Magazine List

We provide information for the magazines from which some of the articles have come, in case you want to subscribe to them.

SUMMARY OF MOTIVE GIFTS

PERCEPTION (PROPHECY) MOTIVE GIFT - THE EYE

Involved in the inspired delivery of warning, exhortation, instruction, judging and making manifest the secrets of the heart.

- Persuasive, sensitive, honest, loyal and responsible.

- Is especially sensitive in perceiving the will of God; he then proclaims it or, depending upon the Lord's leading, prays for it to be accomplished.

- In counsel and prayer: is scripture-based; sees sin clearly and must be careful not to be judgmental.

- In ministry: sees things black or white, with no gray areas; teaches from scripture; his words often bring repentance; prefers teaching older youths and adults.

- In leading a Bible study: spends much time in prayerful preparation; uses Bible as basic text; focuses on subjects like prayer, prophecy and God's will; can't stand sin in people's lives—wants to see complete repentance and change in response to teaching.

Related scripture: Revelation 3:15-16

SERVING MOTIVE GIFT - THE HANDS

Does practical things in order to be of service to others. Receives joy from helping, carrying out instructions, and being of use in a wide variety of ways.

- Helpful, reliable, sensitive, obedient and hard-working.

- Equipped with physical stamina, with disregard for weariness; seems to "see" what needs to be done; is often misunderstood because of the things he does.

- In counsel and prayer: helps others see what needs to be done; prays for the needs of others, wants practical things done for the person prayed for; wants to see God meet a person's needs—sometimes hindering what God is trying to teach and do in that person's life.

- In ministry: makes a good deacon or Sunday school teacher (especially in lower grades); often has a gift of hospitality; enjoys assisting others; e.g., nursery, custodial or secretarial work.

- In leading a Bible study: prefers using prepared materials; does detailed preparation of lessons; focuses on practical subjects that demonstrate faith.

Related scripture: Ephesians 6:7-8

TEACHING MOTIVE GIFT - THE HEAD

Tends to believe that his gift is foundational to the other gifts. Loves to read and study, and places great emphasis on the accuracy of facts and words.

- Comprehending, diligent, perfectionist, dependable.

- May do teaching through writing papers, articles or books rather than teaching in person; may receive more joy from doing research than from presentation.

- In counsel and prayer: wants to clarify truth; prays and ministers using scriptural instruction and explanation.

- In ministry: prefers teaching adult or college-age classes; enjoys preparing and providing enrichment materials; not all people with this gift are called into full-time ministry as teachers.

- In leading a Bible study: wants to prepare own lesson plans; spends much time in biblical research; prefers teaching an entire book of the Bible or a specific topic.

Related scriptures: Hebrews 4:12 and Isaiah 55:11

EXHORTATION MOTIVE GIFT - THE MOUTH

Implores, entreats, consoles and comforts by using life-related experience. Truth is truth for the exhorter—whether it comes from the Bible or experience. Needs to confirm the truth of scripture by experience.

- Loving, obedient and happy.

- Needs the full interest and attention of his listener because the focus of exhorting is the person's personal growth.

- Communicates words of love; when teaching, he aims for the heart and the will, wanting the content to be made effective in people's lives.

- In counsel and prayer: uses prayers of encouragement; prefers to use personal experience; makes an excellent counselor—can pinpoint problems and give helpful step-by-step solutions.

- In ministry: all the motive gifts can teach, but exhorters make learning the most interesting and applicable; is happy teaching any age group, but is especially adept with children and teenagers; usually strong in evangelism.

- In leading a Bible study: prefers using prepared materials; draws from life experiences for illustrations; chooses subjects that help people live victoriously.

Related scripture: Hebrews 10:25

GIVING MOTIVE GIFT - THE ARMS

Lends his strong support as he gives what he has with simplicity, sincerity and liberality.

- Generous, helpful, kind, honest, thrifty, with a well-rounded personality.

- Gives from his earthly possessions with insight about when and whom to help; his giving is not limited to wealth; wants to give practical help; has a love for the Word.

- In counsel and prayer: can help reveal unwise use of assets; has expertise on fund raising and distribution of funds; blesses others with his wisdom.

- In ministry: serves well on advisory boards as an elder or financial adviser; can be adept at teaching any age group—teaches well about giving; often wants to handle finances or promote missionary support.

- In leading a Bible study: enjoys doing his own preparation; tends to gear each lesson to winning someone to Christ; focuses on subjects like evangelism and missions.

Related scripture: Acts 20:35

ADMINISTRATION MOTIVE GIFT - THE SHOULDERS

Provides leadership by working with and through others. Carries responsibility by defining goals and tasks.

- Diligent, capable, responsible, honest and gregarious.

- Helps "maintain" the church by making things easier for others; often holds title of facilitator, organizer, leader or superintendent; likes to see the body of Christ operating smoothly.

- In counsel and prayer: tends to know who or what will work to help an individual reach his potential; can help by pointing out mismanagement of time or recommending procedures which will best accomplish goals; often knows who is to come forth in prayer and ministry; seems to know how to stand in the gap for a specific need when praying.

- In ministry: loves a challenge—to dig in, develop or organize anything he is in charge of; has a creative desire to take raw materials and people to bring something new into existence; is a "jack of all trades, but master of none"—allowing more capable people to carry out the specific tasks.

- In leading a Bible study: Often organizes materials into his own lesson plan; may bring in resource people for added interest; tends to cover broad subjects from different aspects; focuses on teaching or discipling one-on-one.

Related scripture: 1 Corinthians 14:40

COMPASSION (MERCY) MOTIVE GIFT - THE HEART

Shows compassion by word or deed with gentleness, forbearance and joyous abandon. They feel and express God's love.

- Compassionate, loving, caring, helpful and obedient.

- Helps others by empathizing with them and doing good things for them; is quick to detect insincerity, and has trouble with insincere or hard-hearted people; is willing to go the extra mile with someone who is suffering.

- In counsel and prayer: can help discern areas of insensitivity; feels and ministers the heart of God; makes a great intercessor; has a strong desire for unity in the body of Christ and prays accordingly.

- In ministry: Makes a great Sunday school teacher, especially in the primary age group; makes a very compassionate counselor, but can get too emotionally involved with the one he counsels.

- In leading a Bible study: Likes to use prepared materials, but can be spontaneous in his teaching methods; a preferred focus of study is often God's love or having right relationships.

Related scripture: John 15:17

Magazine List

For your convenience we have included the following list of magazines from which this course's articles have been drawn. If you wish to receive these magazines on a regular basis, the subscription information below may help.

Charisma and Christian Life
Subscription Service Department
P.O. Box 420234
Palm Coast, FL 32142-0234

(800) 829-3346
www.charismamag.com

Christ For the Nations
P.O. Box 769000
Dallas, TX 75376-9000

(800) 933-CFNI
www.cfni.org

Decision Magazine
Billy Graham Evangelistic Association
P.O. Box 668886
Harlan, IA 51593-1048

(877) 247-2426
www.billygraham.org
www.billygraham.org/spanish

Discipleship Journal
Subscriber Services
P.O. Box 5548
Harlan, IA 51593-1048

(800)-366-7788
www.navpress.com/dj

Ministry Today
(Formerly Ministries Today)
Magazine Customer Service
600 Rinehart Road
Lake Mary, FL 32746

(407) 333-0600
www.ministrytodaymag.com

Sovereign Grace Ministries
(Formely People of Destiny Int´l,
 then PDI Ministries)
7505 Muncaster Mill Rd
Gaithersburg, MD 20877

(800)-736-2202 or (502)-855-7700
www.sovereigngraceministries.org

Times Square Church Pulpit Series
c/o World Challenge
P.O. Box 260
Lindale, TX 75771

(903) 963-8626
www.worldchallenge.org/en/pulpit_series_newsletter

www.ingramcontent.com/pod-product-compliance
Lightning Source LLC
Chambersburg PA
CBHW081151090426
42736CB00017B/3277